ENDORSEMENTS

My dear friend James Goll has served as a strong prophetic voice in the Body of Christ for decades. He has proven to be a unique gift to the Church and to me personally, excelling in his God-ordained roles as a seasoned prophet, teacher, and writer. His ministry continues to issue the clarion calls of the Holy Spirit—giving us the right-now word from the Father's heart. In the wake of his large collection of writings, James follows up *The Discerner* with another eye-opening look into the prophetic life: *The Prophet*. With his newest book, James extends a bold invitation for the emerging generation of Christ followers to dive unapologetically into the prophetic movement that God is releasing all across the globe. He unpacks a sound biblical framework for prophetic ministry, illuminating the role of prophets with his candid insight and years of wisdom. James is transparent in his assessment of the down-to-earth spiritual dynamics operating in the life of a prophet. His authoritative book elucidates everything that God intended for the prophetic gifts that He has given to His children. *The Prophet* presents a blueprint for you to walk more fully in your prophetic destiny, and James Goll imparts this much-needed message with the grace and power of a true prophet.

Dr. Ché Ahn
President, Harvest International Ministry
Senior Pastor, HROCK Church, Pasadena, CA
International Chancellor, Wagner University

When the Lord speaks, reality gets redefined. What was once impossible becomes possible in the wake of His word. As the conduits of God's presence, the Church has an authority and a responsibility to steward

His voice. James Goll powerfully expounds on this in his new book, *The Prophet*. Perhaps my favorite part is that he reaffirms the value and responsibility of the prophetic for every believer. James offers practical strategies and skills to both develop the personal gift and also release the prophetic gifting to the Body of Christ. As believers, we are called to represent God to a world who is crying out for Him, as He is the desire of the nations. Take courage, press in for more, and pray for wisdom that the whole world would know the goodness of God.

Bill Johnson
Bethel Church, Redding, CA
Author of *The Way of Life* and *Raising Giant-Killers*

I have read many books about "the prophet." I have even written a book about prophets, prophecy, and prophetic revelation. However, I have not read a book that has better explained "the prophet" than James Goll's book, *The Prophet*. James develops the building blocks of the anatomy of a prophetic word and then how that prophetic word is to be delivered. He includes both mind and heart expression in this work. A prophet just does not speak truth but also expresses the heart of God in the delivery of the word. We all prophesy, but some are prophets. This book is a must for either.

In the last four decades we have seen the restoration of the prophet. Thank God that we now have this book that represents the fullness of what this gift was meant to express. We are on the verge of a new Holy Spirit movement. The key to prophecy is the Holy Spirit, and the modern-day prophet must be filled with the Spirit. This book reveals the identity that we are to walk into in the future.

Dr. Chuck D. Pierce
President, Global Spheres Inc.
President, Glory of Zion Intl.

I want to thank Dr. James Goll for writing an amazing book, *The Prophet*, that is practical, inspirational, and most importantly biblical. It is also apologetical in that it refutes the cessationist position, which rejects the continuation of the gift of prophecy and the office of the prophet. I found the book a welcome addition to books about prophecy, but this is more—it is a textbook for anyone who wants to learn about prophecy, prophets, prophetic ministry, and their relationship to the Church in the twenty-first century. The chapter on women and prophecy is a very applicable chapter for the time in which we live, with its high value on women. I also loved the emphasis of the chapter, "From Surrender to Sent Ones" with its focus on being servants and then servant leaders. I believe everyone who wants to grow and learn about prophetic ministry should buy and read *The Prophet*.

Randy Clark, D. Min.
Overseer of the Apostolic Network of Global Awakening,
founder of Global Awakening
President of Global Awakening Theological Seminary
Author of *The Spiritual Gifts Handbook, The Healing Breakthrough,*
Baptized in the Spirit, and *Eyewitness to Miracles*

My friend James Goll never ceases to amaze me with his insight and revelation. This comes from his years of life, experience, and passion of walking with Jesus as his friend. The aroma that is on him impacts you when you are with him. He carries the sweet-smelling savor of his Savior so very well. *The Prophet* as an extension of who he is also carries this. I would encourage you not just to read this book for information, but to let the aroma of the prophetic oil saturate your life. Become inundated with this prophetic essence *that you may all prophesy one by one* (1 Cor. 14:31).

Robert Henderson
Bestselling author of *Operating in the Courts of Heaven* and
The Courts of Heaven Series

The Prophet by Dr. James Goll is a timely and valuable contribution to the church of our generation. We are living in an era when God is truly raising up a great company of His prophets to impact the world with a mighty infusion and invasion of His Kingdom and righteousness. Many might ask questions, such as: what is the difference between being prophetic and being a prophet? Can any believer be a prophet? What qualifies a prophet? Who are the prophets? Can I serve as a prophet? This book will answer those questions and more and will stir hunger in you to embrace the heart and will of God for this hour.

Dr. Patricia King
Founder, Patricia King Ministries

James Goll is a friend and a respected father in the prophetic movement. The message in this new book *The Prophet* is one of the best I have read. It is full of wisdom, anointing, and presence of the Holy Spirit. Once I began to read it, I could not put it down. Within these pages you will encounter a stirred desire to know and hear the voice of the Lord while being activated through the wisdom and instruction of how to prophesy. "But I desire even more that you impart prophetic revelation to others. Greater gain comes through the one who prophesies" (1 Cor. 14:5 The Passion Translation). It is my belief that all who read this book will grow in wisdom and anointing to hear and release the prophetic word of the Lord and that *The Prophet* will become a classic message for years to come. Thank you, James, for this timely word.

Rebecca Greenwood
President and Co-Founder
Christian Harvest International
Strategic Prayer Apostolic Network
Author of *Authority to Tread, Let Our Children Go,
Defeating Strongholds of the Mind, Glory Warfare*

James Goll has given us a book that answers many questions that people frequently ask about the prophetic. This book will help take the whole prophetic movement to a new level.

Dr. Cindy Jacobs
Generals International

James Goll's latest book is a heavenly blueprint of God's unusual spokesmen, the prophets, and their purpose in bringing Kingdom fulfillment into the earth. Like no one else can, James outlines the role of the prophetic in the church—past, present, and future. With a historic as well as apostolic revelation, James gives us a clear vision of God's ultimate goal for Christians in the end-time Church—that all the sons and daughters would prophesy.

The apostle Paul writing to his spiritual sons and daughters in Corinth said, "For though ye have ten thousand instructors in Christ, yet have ye not many fathers: for in Christ Jesus I have begotten you through the gospel" (1 Cor. 4:15 KJV). This book is a twenty-first-century apostolic letter to the Body of Christ from a modern-day prophetic father. It reminds the Church, as Paul did nearly two thousand years ago to his Corinth sons and daughters—eagerly desire the gifts, especially that you will prophesy. I highly recommend *The Prophet* as a must-read for anyone looking to be discipled properly in the prophetic.

Prophet Charlie Shamp
President and co-founder, Destiny Encounters International
Author, *Mystical Prayer*
www.destinyencounters.com

James Goll has been functioning as a prophet for more years than most people even acknowledge the existence of modern-day prophets. He has participated with many different streams and has seen the prophetic gifting manifest in diverse ways throughout the Body of Christ. In his most recent book, *The Prophet*, James gives valuable insight and revelation regarding the function of prophets and prophetic gifts as well as wisdom for those who desire to properly align with the voice of God in today's world. As we are in the time of the second wind of the prophetic movement, this book is vital for those desiring to come up to the next level.

Jane Hamon
Co-apostle of Vision Church @Christian International
Author of *Dreams and Visions, The Deborah Company,
The Cyrus Decree*, and *Discernment*

The book you hold in your hand, *The Prophet*, is both a documentary and a testimonial to the ministry and office of the prophetic. Not only is Dr. James Goll a close friend of mine, but he is an articulate prophetic scribe who historically and practically breaks down the functionality and purpose of the office of the prophet. There is a new breed of prophetic eagle emerging in this generation that will usher in world revival and harvest. James' book, *The Prophet*, will serve as an inspiration and blueprint for all who hunger to move in the depths of the prophetic. I highly recommend this book to all as a must-read.

Dr. Jeff Jansen
Global Fire Ministries International
Senior Leader, Global Fire Church
Author of *Glory Rising, Furious Sound of Glory*, and *Enthroned*
Globalfireministries.com

As I sat down to read through the manuscript of my friend James Goll's new work, *The Prophet*, I became increasingly aware that this was no ordinary book but a significant and timely gift to the Body of Christ. *The Prophet* provides believers with a clear and rich understanding of the many different aspects, challenges, and blessings of prophetic ministry and the office of a prophet. This book will stir, equip, and inspire readers to press into a closer walk with the Lord and to look for more opportunities to share His love through the gift of prophecy. James W. Goll is one of the most well-loved and respected international prophets of our time, and he shares with us in his book *The Prophet* his hard-earned wisdom and experiences as a genuine gift to those called to prophetic ministry. I believe this offering from James Goll will serve as a handbook for prophetic ministry for generations to come as a genuine Christian classic.

Katherine Ruonala
Senior Leader, Glory City Church
Brisbane Australia
Founder and facilitator of the Australian Prophetic Council
Author of *Living in the Miraculous, Wilderness to Wonders,* and
Life with the Holy Spirit
www.katherineruonala.com

James Goll has done it again! I was deeply impacted by *The Seer* and now equally impacted by *The Prophet*. James gives great historical and theological context for those desiring to understand prophecy and the office of the prophet, while also eloquently making applicable the teachings to all believers. I believe that as this book fills the shelves of churches and equipping centers around the world, many will find themselves embracing their call into the office of the prophet and many more will embrace the culture of the prophetic.

Johnathan Stidham
JS Ministries
Co-author of *The Seer Realms*

My friend and both spiritual and prophetic papa, Dr. James Goll, brings a grace to the Body of Christ in his new book, *The Prophet*. James has a unique ability to be both a prophet and one who equips, bringing the Church into alignment to walk in a prophetic lifestyle. His ability to stir up the gift within a generation is key as the Lord releases prophetic voices that will inspire and build the Body for such a time as this. I believe we have entered into a second wave of prophetic grace and a fresh outpouring of Holy Spirit revelation to the Church so that we can represent well the Lord as we make love the goal. James' book *The Prophet* is very timely and will be a blessing to this multi-generational move of the Spirit. Be prepared to go to the next level in hearing and releasing your prophetic voice.

Steven Springer
International speaker
President and co-founder, Global Presence Ministries
Senior leader, Global Presence Center
Apostolic overseer, Global Presence Apostolic Network

If you are a prophetic person or desire to increase your flow of prophecy you must read James Goll's new book, *The Prophet*. This may be his best book yet! Not only does he share amazing insights into the history of prophetic ministry, but he brilliantly lays out how to both receive and release this gift in your own life. You'll learn insights into different modes of prophetic communication, making your own prophetic ministry more developed and accurate. I know this book will have a deep and lasting impact on you as you grow into the prophetic voice God is calling you to be.

Matt Sorger
Matt Sorger Ministries
Prophetic Healing Minister, Author, Mentor
mattsorger.com

I have known and ministered extensively with James Goll for over 25 years. In this book he shows his wealth of understanding of the history, the purpose, and the various ways the prophetic ministry is to correctly operate. It would be impossible for me to honestly endorse this book based on the academic prowess of the content alone; I really personally know this man, and his heart for all to be enriched with true prophetic anointing. One of the most powerful aspects of James's ministry is: Activation. I have been present when it has ignited gifts and even initiated powerful moves of the Holy Spirit that have spread like a tsunami. Please consider doing this, put his name on your refrigerator and pray for him, often. May you receive the Prophet's reward.

Mickey Robinson
co-founder: Prophetic Destiny International
Author, Speaker, and Friend

THE PROPHET

DESTINY IMAGE BOOKS BY
JAMES W. GOLL

Empowered Prayer Intercession: The Power and Passion to Shape History

James W. Goll 365-Day Personal Prayer Guide

Prayer Storm

Prayer Storm Study Guide

Shifting Shadows of Supernatural Experiences
(co-authored with Julia Loren)

The Call of the Elijah Revolution
(co-authored with Lou Engle)

The Seer (and *The Seer Expanded*)

The Seer Devotional Journal Discovering the Seer in You

The Lost Art of Intercession

The Lost Art of Practicing His Presence

The Lost Art of Pure Worship
(co-authored with Chris DuPre')

Exploring the Nature and Gift of Dreams

Exploring Your Dreams and Visions

DESTINY IMAGE BOOKS BY
JAMES W. GOLL AND MICHAL ANN GOLL

Adventures in the Prophetic
(co-authored with Mickey Robinson, Patricia King,
Jeff Jansen and Ryan Wyatt)

Compassion: A Call to Take Action (Women on the Frontlines)

*Dream Language: The Prophetic Power of Dreams,
Revelations, and the Spirit of Wisdom*

God Encounters

God Encounters Today

The Call to the Secret Place (Women on the Frontlines)

THE

PROPHET

CREATING AND SUSTAINING
A LIFE-GIVING
PROPHETIC CULTURE

JAMES W. GOLL

DESTINY IMAGE® PUBLISHERS, INC.
P.O. Box 310, Shippensburg, PA 17257-0310
"Promoting Inspired Lives."

This book and all other Destiny Image and Destiny Image Fiction books are available at Christian bookstores and distributors worldwide.

Cover design by Eileen Rockwell

For more information on foreign distributors, call 717-532-3040.

Reach us on the Internet: www.destinyimage.com.

ISBN 13 TP: 978-0-7684-5047-7

ISBN 13 eBook: 978-0-7684-5045-3

ISBN 13 HC: 978-0-7684-5044-6

ISBN 13 LP: 978-0-7684-5046-0

For Worldwide Distribution, Printed in the U.S.A.

HC: 1 2 3 4 5 6 7 8 / 23 22 21 20 19

TP: 1 2 3 4 5 6 7 8 / 23 22 21 20 19

DEDICATION

For years I have placed a high value upon teaching and encouraging young leaders in the global prayer and prophetic movements. I am now seeing what I have prayed into for years, the joining of the generations. It is such a joy to see these young eagles come forth, carrying the seven spirits of God into the seven cultural spheres of society.

With this in mind, I want to dedicate this book, *The Prophet*, to the young prophetic voices that are emerging across the planet for such a time as this. To all of you: May my "ceiling" truly be your "floor"!

ACKNOWLEDGMENTS

With a deep gratitude and appreciation I want to thank Larry Sparks of Destiny Image for offering me the opportunity to publish *The Prophet*, in hopes that it might become a modern-day classic. When he first proposed the idea, I prayed a short prayer and responded in the affirmative: "Absolutely! Yes! What an honor!"

Any work I do is always a team effort. I might be the team leader, but close behind me is the resilient Kathy Deering. This devoted woman of God has been my writing assistant on more books than I can recall. Her faithfulness and diligence in researching and rearranging my content for greater cohesive flow is a gift to me and thus to the Body of Christ at large.

I am also deeply indebted to those fathers in the prophetic who have impacted my life for so many years. These include the late John Sanford and Bob Jones as well as the elderly statesman, Paul Cain. I especially want to acknowledge the wisdom, consistency, and character of Bishop Bill Hamon, founder of Christian International. I thank the Lord that I have been privileged to walk in the shadows of these dear men of God.

Would that all the Lord's people were prophets, that the Lord would put His Spirit upon them!

NUMBERS 11:29

CONTENTS

FOREWORD

I was sitting on a plane and I had about 20 text messages come through, each one a more important testimony or story than the last about how different friends had encountered actual prophets in our day who gave them prophetic words. These words all had stories attached and each prophet had brought different people into a place of great authority and connection in their sphere of society. Each one was a testimony of how the prophet had affected their life and how the outcome was forever different because of the word they had received. I was so excited because it wasn't just spiritual encouragement. I heard them talking about different men and women whom God is raising up or has raised up as prophets and how prophets are alive and well in our time. I then heard clearly in my spirit that God is restoring the dignity of prophets in our time.

Prophets in the Old Testament were the most sought-after people when anyone faced transition, crises, or national purposes in Israel and beyond. The prophets were the hosts of God's thoughts, and when people met with them this very omnipresent God made an appearance through His prophets in a way that proved that He cared very deeply about those who sought after Him.

In the New Testament we see the prophets carry another equally important role—to help establish God's Kingdom in all the world. They were the ones who helped the rest of Christians navigate their revelation and prophetic journey. The world is so hungry for the divine counsel of the Holy Spirit who, when you meet with Him, what normally takes a year of counseling, an expensive business coach, a life coach, or an educational process can happen in a moment.

Think about the multi-billion dollar industry of psychics, new age, mediums, and the occult. Why are they so present in society? Because people are looking for spiritual guidance. People are hungry for spiritual truth that they can apply to their pain, their careers, their identities. This is such a counterfeit to the ministry of prophets who bring a connection to God's original plans and intentions in real time through the Spirit of God. And He does it free through His prophets!

James Goll is like a master encyclopedia of the prophetic in our generation and he has released this book that helps reestablish the theology of prophets for our time. His in-depth teaching approach to a very controversial subject has created an on-ramp for everyone who is hungry to understand prophets and their role for the church today. His materials mentor and train and are as great in perspective as they are in education. This book will give you an edge in the prophetic that the world needs right now. It will help shape the culture of how you engage your sphere of influence in the prophetic and will give you courage biblically to pursue your calling. It will also help you understand some of the hardships that prophets face as well as give you insight for the different ways revelation comes.

James has unlimited experience as a prophet that is so rare and that makes this book different. He also takes his time fleshing out the role biblically but also uses his experience to point the way. Ultimately we want to see the role of a prophet have its rightful place in the Church because it acts like having a full bank account—it is a resource we can't live without once we experience it. It adds grace to situations and accelerates everything we do when we can divinely place prophets in their authority and in relationship.

Read this book; let it fashion the role of prophet into your theology and heart so that you can pursue the healthiest form and we can restore the office of the prophet.

Shawn Bolz
Bestselling author of *Translating God* and *God Secrets*
www.bolzministries.com

INTRODUCTION

J ames Goll's book has brought much understanding and insight to the ministry of the prophet. I am always happy when someone prints a book promoting the life and ministry of the prophet. I have functioned as a prophet since 1953. However, I was functioning under the Body of Christ's concepts of what a prophet could do. In 1973 God gave me a divine visitation and revelation of the ministry of God's twentieth-century prophet. I was anointed to prophesy to numerous people in one evening of ministry. Then an older prophet in 1984 prophesied to me that God was anointing me to be a prophet who would be a reproducer of reproducers who would reproduce more prophetic ministries. I wrote the *Manual for Ministering Spiritual Gifts* from which we have trained almost a half-million saints over the last 30 years in every continent. After the prophetic movement was birthed in 1988, I wrote three books, *Prophets and Personal Prophecy, Prophets and the Prophetic Movement, Prophets, Pitfalls, and Principles* to show the validity of prophetic in the twentieth century. These three books explain the prophetic movement and the pitfalls to avoid and principles to practice.

James Goll pioneered what he called the "seer prophets" and has demonstrated the ministry of seer prophets. Like most true prophets he has gone through many trials and tests plus the suffering of his wife's death and fighting cancer in his body. He has shown himself to be a real warrior, overcomer, and faithful servant of the Lord. I have known and fellowshipped with James for several years. He has proven to be a true man of God and a true friend.

May this book help many to accept and understand the calling and ministry of God's prophets in the twenty-first century.

Bishop Bill Hamon
Bishop, Christian International Apostolic-Global Network
Author: *The Eternal Church*
Prophets and Personal Prophecy
Prophets and the Prophetic Movement
Prophets, Pitfalls, and Principles
Apostles/Prophets and the Coming Moves of God
The Day of the Saints
Who Am I and Why Am I Here
Prophetic Scriptures Yet to be Fulfilled
70 Reasons for Speaking in Tongues
How Can These Things Be? God's Weapons of War

FOR THE MANY,
NOT THE FEW

I am firmly convinced that the current prophetic empowering is intended for the many, for the rank and file "ordinary" members of the Body of Christ, not just the few, the prophetic "superstars." Successive waves of God's Spirit will continue to unfold until Christ's Church has been saturated with the spirit of wisdom and of revelation in the knowledge of Him (see Eph. 1:17). Our Father God will not let up until His people are filled with the revelation of the loveliness of His Son. If that sounds inviting, you will know it's for you!

Moses came into this understanding in his day. The pressures on this anointed man were tremendous as he tried to lead his complaining people into the Promised Land. His cry to the Lord is found in Numbers 11:14, where he lamented, "I alone am not able to carry all this people, because it is too burdensome for me." But God had a solution to Moses' dilemma:

> *Gather for Me seventy men from the elders of Israel, whom you know to be the elders of the people and their officers and bring them to the tent of meeting and let them take their*

stand there with you. Then I will come down and speak with
you there, and I will take of the Spirit who is upon you, and
will put Him upon them; and they shall bear the burden
of the people with you, so that you will not bear it all alone
(NUM. 11:16–17).

So Moses went out and told the people the words of the Lord. He gathered the seventy elders and stationed them around the tent. Then the Lord came down in the cloud and He took of the Spirit who was upon Moses and placed Him upon the seventy elders. Verse 25 tells us, and it came about that "when the Spirit rested upon them, they prophesied. But they did not do it again."

What a beautiful depiction, yet what an unfulfilling outcome! With a stroke of the Master's hand, the prophetic presence that rested upon Moses was distributed among the seventy and they prophesied, but after that they did not do it again. Thank God this was not the final word on the matter.

Two men had remained in the camp, Medad and Eldad. They had not shown up at the right place at the right time. Nonetheless, the Spirit came upon them as He had done upon the elders, and they released the Spirit in the camp. As I envision this scene, I see two desperate warriors, so hungry for the Lord's anointing that their heart cry to a compassionate God was "Give me all you've got! More Lord!" God answered their plea. There is no indication that Medad and Eldad ever quit prophesying. Perhaps they went wildly through camp laying hands on people and declaring God's mighty Word.

Maybe it seemed a little unusual and out of order, because a young man ran and told Moses, "Eldad and Medad are prophesying in the camp!" (v. 27). Joshua also got into the act, adding, "Moses, my lord, restrain them!" (v. 28). Isn't this reaction similar to those who through the ages have wanted to control the activity of the Spirit?

But Moses said to him, "Are you jealous for my sake? Would that all the Lord's people were prophets, that the Lord would put His Spirit upon them" (Num. 11:29).

God's heart is revealed through Moses' answer. The prophetic spirit is for the many, not the few. The seventy elders at the tent prophesied only once. God's yearning is for a generation of faceless people to arise with a continuous abiding of His prophetic presence.

Centuries later the prophet Joel picked up God's trumpet and declared that in the last days God would pour out His Spirit upon all flesh (see Joel 2:28). Peter, on the day of Pentecost, took up the baton from Joel and proclaimed, "Your sons and your daughters shall prophesy, and your young men shall see visions and your old men shall dream dreams" (Acts 2:17).

Do you see? The prophetic spirit is for the many, not the few! Reach out and lift your own cry to Him: "Father, pour out Your Spirit upon the Body of Your Son to such a degree that we will be propelled beyond the tent of meeting into the marketplace of our day. As You did with Medad and Eldad, release the abundance of the spirit of wisdom and revelation and enable Your many people to give the testimony of Jesus through the Spirit of prophecy."

Ultimately, that is what *The Prophet* is all about—capturing the heart of Jesus and speaking forth His thoughts even as you continue to become grounded and established with a firm biblical foundation.

To help guide you through, this book is broken down into four sections: Prophetic Beginnings, Prophetic Development, Prophetic Diversity, and Prophetic Commissioning. Each of the twelve chapters builds on the previous one.

May the Lord's blessing be with you. May He lay a firm foundation of the testimony of Jesus in your life!

PART ONE

PROPHETIC BEGINNINGS

CHAPTER 1

WHERE EAGLES
DARE TO FLY

Those who wait for the Lord will gain new strength; they will mount up with wings like eagles, they will run and not get tired, they will walk and not become weary.

ISAIAH 40:31

L ike John the beloved on the Isle of Patmos, I hear the voice of the Spirit saying, *"Come up here. Come up higher."* Yes, soar like an eagle above the powers of darkness and evil principalities. Rise above into an atmosphere free from spiritual warfare, contention, care, and worry. Catch the wind and be carried higher as the current freely flows and even a whisper of a breeze causes you to gain elevation. Oh, how the mighty eagle dares to fly where no two-winged creature has ever flown before.

The prophet, like the eagle, flies higher and sees further than all of God's gifted ones. The prophet soars through the open door and rises into the place where the sky is blue, the vision is clear, and your sight is filled with third-heavenly views. As prophets, prophetically gifted people, and the long-awaited prophetic generation of courageous believers come forth, you know that the Father's glorious purposes are accelerating for such a time as this.

A Variety of Eagles

More than sixty species of majestic eagles are found worldwide—Eurasia, Africa, Central and South America, Australia, Canada, and the United States, where in 1782 the American Bald Eagle was adopted as the national emblem. An eagle's wingspan can reach 7½ feet (228 cm) and their nests can weigh 1,000 pounds (453 kg). Although solitary birds, they mate for life. Eagles have long been symbols of grandeur and power and have appeared on currency, seals, military insignia, and flags from ancient to current times.

Not only have eagles been the subject of Egyptian, Roman, and Native American folklore, eagles are also found throughout the Bible's Old Testament and in the book of Revelation; have you noticed? God uses examples of eagles to teach us many things. He compares us and this amazing bird—if only we choose to rely on His strength for everything.

The passage above from Isaiah is preceded by these verses:

Do you not know? Have you not heard?
The Everlasting God, the Lord,
the Creator of the ends of the earth
Does not become weary or tired.
His understanding is inscrutable.
He gives strength to the weary,
And to him who lacks might He increases power.
Though youths grow weary and tired,

And vigorous young men stumble badly,

Yet those who wait for the Lord

Will gain new strength... (ISA. 40:29–31).

Our all-sufficient Creator does not leave us on our own any more than a mother eagle leaves her chicks on their own. And He cares for us in every way, anticipating our weaknesses and putting fresh wind under our wings day after day and year after year.

In this book I want to lead you on an exploration of how God equips His own sons and daughters to soar all the way up to the sun (Son), as they tirelessly prophesy His glory in multiple ways. He is the one "who satisfies your years [or desires] with good things, so that your youth is renewed like the eagle" (Ps. 103:5).

As we follow the Lord and follow His call, we can certainly get weary. He wants to show us how to have both of our wings ready—the Word of God and worshipful prayer—so that when the wind of the Spirit comes in force, we can climb up and draw beautiful circles as we wheel in the sky.

Everywhere in Scripture, eagles represent swiftness and strength—and the glory of God. I remember the eagles in both Ezekiel's heavenly visitation and then, centuries later, in John's revelation:

As for the form of their faces, each had the face of a man; all four had the face of a lion on the right and the face of a bull on the left, and all four had the face of an eagle (EZEK. 1:10).

The first living creature was like a lion, the second living creature like a calf, the third living creature had a face like a man, and the fourth living creature was like a flying eagle. The four living creatures, each having six wings, were full of eyes around and within. And they do not rest day or night, saying: "Holy, holy, holy,

Lord God Almighty,

Who was and is and is to come!"

Whenever the living creatures give glory and honor and
thanks to Him who sits on the throne, who lives forever and
ever (Rev. 4:7–9, nkjv).

Some Bible commentators say that these four faces or four living creatures refer to the four Gospels, each of which depicts a different aspect of
the nature of God. With one voice, what do these creatures do in Heaven?
They proclaim, "Holy, holy, holy is the Lord God Almighty." They just can't
stop telling of His glory. And as we ourselves mount up on eagles' wings,
borne higher and higher by the wind of His Spirit, neither can we.

Eagles as a Prophetic Symbol

The eagle is one of the biggest and certainly the most majestic of all
living birds. This is why so many countries, no less than twenty-five of
them, depict eagles in their coat of arms. North American native tribes use
eagle feathers in their religious lives. Here in North America, we are most
familiar with the golden eagle and the bald eagle (which is not really bald,
of course, although some of us can identify with that, too!). The writers
of Scripture would have seen golden eagles, along with three other kinds
of eagles, and more during migration seasons. Mature eagles have come
to be admired the world over as living symbols of freedom, power, and
transcendence.

Eagles are often considered specifically representative of the prophetic
anointing. People who make lists of scriptural symbolism always interpret eagles this way—just think about the proverbial sharp-sightedness of
eagles, not to mention their capacity to "come up higher."

Eagles are even more meaningful to me. For years the combined ministries of Encounters Network and Compassion Acts served the Cherokee

Nation headquartered in Tahlequah, Oklahoma with acts of kindness, humanitarian aid, and prayer. Because of this connection, I was adopted by the Cherokee tribe and given the name "White Eagle" during a special day of prayer. I was honored in a ceremony, presented with a long white eagle feather, and commissioned to "soar into the heavens" in prayer and prophecy.

I call the late Bob Jones, one of my prophetic mentors, my "prophetic papa." He was known as a seer, and he wore this one sweatshirt all the time. Maybe he had ten of them; I would not know for sure. Anyway, his blue sweatshirt had the picture of an eagle on it. Nothing could have been more appropriate. Bob had been commissioned as an eagle who would call forth and equip the eagles who would in turn equip more eagles for the next two or three generations.

As prophetic people, we need to "come up higher," and see things from a heavenly perspective. The apostle John declared prophetically:

> *After this I looked, and there before me was a door standing open in heaven. And the voice I had first heard speaking to me like a trumpet said, "Come up here, and I will show you what must take place after this." At once I was in the Spirit, and there before me was a throne in heaven with someone sitting on it. And the one who sat there had the appearance of jasper and ruby. A rainbow that shone like an emerald encircled the throne* (Rev. 4:1–3, NIV).

Each of us must catch the vision that God sends, because while not all of us are meant to have a public prophetic ministry, each of us can prophesy in particular ways. Together, we are called to be the prophetic Body of Christ. Our God invites us to come and see the world and His Kingdom from a higher, heavenly perspective.

It is not only about the next great experience. It is about keeping on looking, as John the Beloved did. He kept on looking until he saw the Lord Jesus enthroned.

EAGLES AND US

When you look at the facts about eagles, you can see all kinds of parallels with prophetic expression. Let's look at some of them, keeping in mind the wisdom of Paul: "However, the spiritual is not first, but the natural, and afterward the spiritual" (1 Cor. 15:46, NKJV). Remember: first the natural, then the spiritual. The spiritual does not come first.

There are over sixty species of eagles in the world. Undoubtedly, there are over sixty "species" of prophets and prophetic expression in the world, too. Prophets come in all shapes and sizes and, as you will see in the chapters of this book, they express God's heart and mind in a wide variety of ways.

As you may remember, fifty years ago bald eagles in North America used to be on the endangered species list, since only about five hundred breeding pairs were thought to exist. About ten years ago, they were removed from the list, and now enjoy a "protected" status. I see some similarities with what has happened to prophetic voices in the Church. Once in danger of extinction, the importance of the prophetic has now been restored and elevated in status, at least in many places. In fact, it happened over the course of that same fifty-year period, in both cases starting in 1967.

When I first started out ministering in the Body of Christ, prophecy was unusual. It was a big deal and many Christians did not think it was valid. Now, along with the wide range of acceptable worship styles, many people who used to try to avoid anything labeled "prophetic" now welcome it. In 1967—the same year that the bald eagle was put on the endangered species list—three important movements in the Church came into being: the charismatic movement, the Jesus People movement, and the Messianic movement. Back in 1967, there were not very many "eagles" flying in the Church. Oh, that eagles would multiply in the Church, that they would continue to be no longer endangered, but rather protected!

It is a natural fact: Eagles can out-fly and out-hunt many other species, and they take advantage of the food sources they have at hand. They may have a big range to cover, and they stay within it once they mature. They fly so high in the sky that they seem to come from a heavenly realm when they plunge to earth in their single-minded pursuit of their prey. I think you can see how this might be analogous to prophets!

Most eagles mate for life, and the males and females look quite similar to each other. After constructing large nests with care, they maintain them for their two or three chicks each season (taking turns feeding the chicks and passing on to the next generation what they need to know). Some eagles build their nests in tall trees. Others, like the golden eagle in Israel, build on inaccessible cliffs:

> *The eagle mounts up*
> *And makes his nest on high.*
> *On the cliff he dwells and lodges,*
> *Upon the rocky crag, an inaccessible place.*
> *From there he spies out food;*
> *His eyes see it from afar* (JOB 39:27–29).

From such heights, they can catch the wind currents and soar even higher—or plummet to earth at fantastic speed to capture the prey that their "eagle eyes" have spotted. As prophetic people, we too hope to be able to start high, having nested and rested, from there to catch the wind currents of the Holy Spirit. From such a high perspective, our God-given spiritual sight can spot a target that other eyes would miss. We can see the enemy, and we can see provision.

Did you know that eagles can see more colors than humans can? We can see the three primary colors, red, blue, and yellow, and their gradations. But eagles can distinguish more colors, including those in the UV range, which helps them follow invisible-to-humans urine trails of small animals.

More about eagles' vision: The eyes of big eagles are about the same size as human eyes, but their vision is up to four times as sharp as human twenty-twenty vision. This means that an eagle can spot prey over several miles from a souring altitude of a thousand feet. Do prophets seem to have extra-sharp vision as well? I believe they do.

Over the years many preachers have stated (based on the passage below) that a mother eagle will push her fledgling eaglet out of the nest before it is able to fly, swooping underneath to carry it back to a solid perch:

> *Like an eagle that stirs up its nest,*
> *That hovers over its young,*
> *He spread His wings and caught them,*
> *He carried them on His pinions* (DEUT. 32:11).

This is poetic language, a beautiful picture of the way God teaches us to "fly" in the Spirit, and it goes along with the rest of our prophetic analogy. Naturalists know it does not really happen, although the eagle parents do shield their young with their strong wings as the prior verse portrays:

> *In a desert land he found him,*
> *in a barren and howling waste.*
> *He shielded him and cared for him;*
> *he guarded him as the apple of his eye...* (DEUT. 32:10, NIV).

Eagles never look back over their shoulders or worry about competitors. They are beautifully confident and highly focused. Remember what Jesus said about putting your hand to the plow and not looking back? (See Luke 9:61–62.)[1]

BIRTHRIGHT

Andrew Murray, prolific South African writer-pastor of the early twentieth century, once composed a book called *With Wings as Eagles*. In it, he stated:

> How did the eagle get its wings? By its birth. It was born a royal eagle. It has royal descent.... We are all born with eagle wings; we have within us a divine nature; we have within us the very Spirit of Christ Jesus to draw us heavenward.[2]

Regardless of whether or not you think of yourself as a prophet, that is what you are. You have a connection with Heaven that you can renew on a daily basis. You can bring Heaven to earth through your words and actions. You are called to fly higher. As an eternal being, you have been called to dwell in the heavenlies. You—yes, you!—have been called to mount up with eagles' wings so that you can bring Heaven to your little patch of the earth.

The prophet Jeremiah mentioned "...your nest as high as an eagle's" (Jer. 49:16). Obadiah wrote, "you soar like the eagle and make your nest among the stars" (Obad. 1:4, NIV). It is your birthright to dwell on the heights with God. Your position is with Him, so choose to occupy it! He raises you up to the highest heights, so do not be foolish or negligent or rebellious and forfeit your glorious position with Him.

"Be still, and know that I am God!" said the psalmist (Ps. 46:10, NKJV). You do not have to be intense to be a prophet. You can move from the natural to the spiritual in a really *natural* way. An eagle waits for the perfect time to launch into the air currents so that he can ascend without flapping unnecessarily. Be still and just wait for that perfect moment, which will come in its season. Eagles do not fly high all the time, and neither should you.

The most powerful prophetic words are relational, not professional. Reaching out with acts of kindness may be the best prophetic ministry of all, and you certainly do not have to punctuate every word with "thus saith the Lord." Feel free to change your language, making it less religious and more ordinary, more approachable. I will have much more to say about this as the following chapters unfold.

Let love be your aim (see 1 Cor. 14:1). Love is the conduit that carries faith. You do not have to be a know-it-all. Just be a genuine person who cares about people. Ask questions and get to know people. Learn to move in the gifts of the Spirit as you grow in the fruit of the Spirit (love, joy, peace, patience, kindness, gentleness, and self-control—see Galatians 5:22–23).

It is a process. Like an eaglet, you were not hatched knowing how to soar or hunt. Even when you reach maturity, you will have to learn new things. Just remember that you have the best Teacher you could possibly have, and that He has promised to perfect the work He has begun in you (see Phil. 1:6). He will also recondition you all along the way, much like the way He reconditions the feathers of a molting eagle.

Never forget your goal, which is the goal for anyone who is called by His name: to exalt Jesus. After John was invited into the heavenly throne room, he recorded these words: "The testimony of Jesus is the spirit of prophecy" (Rev. 19:10, NKJV). What is important is not the sweep of your wingspan or the accuracy of your eye. What matters is that you train your eagle eyes to keep your focus on Jesus Himself. As an eagle of God, are you releasing His testimony?

LET'S PRAY

Father, in Jesus' great name, we want to see a prophetic company
rise up with their hearts set on You. Help us to pursue love and yet
earnestly desire the gift of prophecy. Give us prophetic hearts so

that we can release the testimony of Jesus to all those with whom we come into contact. May we have the eyes of eagles to discern our prey and learn to swoop down for the capture. Increase our wingspan so that we can soar to new heights. We declare that we are no longer an endangered species and that we do not have to live in fear. Yes, like the eagles, we now dare to fly higher than ever before! Amen.

CHAPTER 2

THE HISTORY OF PROPHETIC MINISTRY

God has spoken by the mouth of all His holy prophets since the world began.

ACTS 3:21, NKJV

G od has spoken through His prophetic voice since the time of the Creation. God is still speaking today. It is His very nature to communicate with His people. The writers of the Gospels and the epistles of the New Testament made various references to the "prophets of old," building on the foundation that continued to be laid for centuries:

Rejoice and be glad, because great is your reward in heaven, for in the same way they persecuted the prophets who were before you (MATT. 5:12, NIV).

You say, "If we had lived in the days of our ancestors, we would not have taken part with them in shedding the blood of the prophets."...Therefore I am sending you prophets and sages and teachers. Some of them you will kill and crucify; others you will flog in your synagogues and pursue from town to town. And so upon you will come all the righteous blood that has been shed on earth, from the blood of righteous Abel to the blood of Zechariah son of Berekiah, whom you murdered between the temple and the altar (MATT. 23:30, 34–35, NIV).

He spoke by the mouth of His holy prophets from of old (LUKE 1:70).

You will have a great reward awaiting you in heaven. And you will be in good company—the ancient prophets were treated that way [persecuted] *too!* (LUKE 6:23, TLB)

This Good News was promised long ago by God's prophets in the Old Testament (ROM. 1:2, TLB).

But the things which God announced beforehand by the mouth of all the prophets, that His Christ would suffer, He has thus fulfilled. Therefore repent and return, so that your sins may be wiped away, in order that times of refreshing may come from the presence of the Lord; and that He may send Jesus, the Christ appointed for you, whom heaven must receive until the period of restoration of all things about which God spoke by the mouth of His holy prophets from ancient time. Moses said, "The Lord God will raise up for you a prophet like me from your brethren; to Him you shall give heed to everything He says to you. And it will be that every soul that does not heed that prophet shall be utterly destroyed from among the people." And likewise, all the prophets who have spoken, from

Samuel and his successors onward, also announced these days.
It is you who are the sons of the prophets and of the covenant
which God made with your fathers, saying to Abraham, "And
in your seed all the families of the earth shall be blessed." For
you first, God raised up His Servant and sent Him to bless
you by turning every one of you from your wicked ways (ACTS
3:18–26).

Those prophets of old were not only the ones who have books of the
Bible named after them. Luke makes reference to Abel as a prophet: "Therefore this generation will be held responsible for the blood of all the prophets that has been shed since the beginning of the world, from the blood of
Abel to the blood of Zechariah, who was killed between the altar and the
sanctuary" (Luke 11:50–51, NIV; see also Gen. 4:4, 10). That is one of the
places in Scripture where the inevitable suffering of prophets is mentioned.

Even the prophet Jeremiah, who is now considered a premier "prophet
of old" himself, referred back to his predecessors when he said, "The prophets who were before me and before you from ancient times prophesied
against many lands and against great kingdoms, of war and of calamity and
of pestilence" (Jer. 28:8). Not concerned only with his own generation, he
recognized that he was part of a long line of prophets who had spoken into
the history of the world. Far from confining themselves to speaking to the
religious people and institutions, they spoke to the culture around them.

All along, God keeps looking for prophets with an edge, for those
whose perspective comes from beyond their human limitations. He looks
for "prophetic solutionists" who can deliver God's answer to problems that
are impossible to solve by human wisdom and effort alone.

The prophetic task is not yet complete, and it will not be complete
"until we all come to the unity of the faith" as we see here:

He Himself gave some to be apostles, some prophets, some
evangelists, and some pastors and teachers, for the equipping of

the saints for the work of ministry, for the edifying of the body of Christ, till we all come to the unity of the faith and of the knowledge of the Son of God, to a perfect man, to the measure of the stature of the fullness of Christ (EPH. 4:11–13, NKJV).

Obviously, this has not yet occurred. Yet at the perfect moment, the second coming of the Lord Jesus Christ will occur, when the Father will "send Jesus"—to repeat the words from above—"the Christ appointed for you, whom heaven must receive until the period of restoration of all things about which God spoke by the mouth of His holy prophets from ancient time" (Acts 3:20–21).

Regardless of whether you are male or female, you are one of the "sons of the prophets" (see Acts 3:25) who has been appointed to help restore the Kingdom of God in the earth. It does not matter so much what your spiritual gifts are as it does how you are living out your calling to *be* a gift, in His name. At the same time, it is of vital importance to recognize that not one of the five-fold ministry gifts— apostle, prophet, evangelist, pastor, and teacher—has been retired. Many Christians believe that today we see only the gifts of pastor, teacher, and evangelist in full operation, but not the gifts of prophet or apostle. I would argue from this passage that all five ministry gifts will be needed straight through history until the end. How else will we get there in one piece?

PROPHETS BEFORE CHRIST

The clearest way to give you the history of prophecy at a glance is to break down the centuries into specific eras of prophetic activity, listing the representative prophets whose names will be familiar to you:

Pre-Patriarchal Prophets (4000–1450 B.C.—before Moses)

+ Abel (Luke 11:50–51)

+ Enoch (Jude 14–15; recorded in Genesis 5:18, 21)

+ Noah (Heb. 11:7; 1 Pet. 3:20; Gen. 9:25–27; prophesied concerning the flood and his own descendants)

Patriarchal Prophets

+ Abraham (Gen. 20:7; Ps. 105:9–15)

+ Joseph (prophesied regarding the future exodus from Egypt in Genesis 50:24–25)

+ Others include Isaac and Jacob.

Prophets of the Mosaic Period (1450–1050 B.C.)

+ Moses ("There has never been another prophet like Moses, for the Lord talked to him face to face." Deut. 34:10, TLB)

+ Miriam—the first woman prophet mentioned in Scripture (Exod. 15:20)

+ Deborah (Judg. 4:4)

+ Others include Aaron and Hannah.

Prophets of the Early Monarchy (1050–931 B.C.)

The prophetic plea was mainly national; it spoke of repentance and conversion.

+ Samuel (1 Sam. 1; Acts 3:24)

+ Nathan (2 Sam. 7:2–17; 1 Kings 1:8–45)

+ Gad the seer (1 Sam. 22:5; 1 Chron. 21:9–19)

+ David (Acts 1:16; 2:29–31; 4:25)

Prophets of the Divided Monarchy (931–845 B.C.)

- Ahijah (1 Kings 11:29–32; a prophetic action regarding the division of the kingdom)

- Jehu (1 Kings 16:1–7)

- Elijah (1 Kings 17; 2 Kings 1)

- Elisha (2 Kings 2–13)

- Others include Shemaiah, Iddo, Jehaziel, Hanani, Zechariah, and Micaiah.

Prophets of Canonical Period (845–400 B.C.)

The prophets urged repentance for the divided kingdom. Certain prophets and their writings became accepted as part of the canon of Scripture. The apocalyptic thrust and the revelation of the future Church developed.

- Pre-Exile: Obadiah, Joel, Jonah, Amos, Hosea, Micah, Isaiah, Jeremiah, Nahum, Zephaniah, and Habakkuk

- Exile: Ezekiel and Daniel

- Post-Exile: Haggai, Zechariah, and Malachi

Prophets of the Inter-Advent Period (400 B.C.–A.D. 33)

- John the Baptist (Luke 1:76)

- Zacharias (Luke 1:67)

- Anna, a prophetess (Luke 2:36)

- Jesus Christ (John 6:14; Luke 4:24; see also Isa. 61:1)

New Testament Church Prophets (A.D. 33–100)

- Numerous anonymous prophets (Acts 11:27)

- Agabus (Acts 11:27–28)

- Certain prophets with teachers (Acts 13:1; This list could include Barnabas, Simeon [Niger], Lucius of Cyrene, and Manaen.)

- Judas and Silas (Acts 15:32; It seems evident that some of the apostles also functioned prophetically as well, i.e. John, Paul, and others.)

Most of these people were not known as prophets until others could see the fruit of their lives. Over time and in various ways, they spoke for God and people noticed. That is how it works for every gift of the Spirit. As you are faithful in the small, hidden tasks, God sees fit to promote you to more. Faithfulness brings increase.

Early on in my own life, I found myself prophesying. In fact, the first prophecy I ever heard came out of my own mouth. I prophesied before I ever prayed or spoke in public or worshiped in tongues. Does that mean I was commissioned as a prophet? No, I became a pastor. In that role, I ended up becoming a teacher. My goal was to be a good one, which takes a lot of work and time. Now I am essentially a pastor to pastors and a teacher to prophets. I think it is wonderful and interesting how God leads us over a lifetime.

SCHOOLS OF THE PROPHETS

Starting with Samuel, we see schools of prophets portrayed in Scripture.

"...As you arrive there you will meet a band of prophets coming down the hill playing a psaltery, a timbrel, a flute, and a harp, and prophesying as they come:

"At that time the Spirit of the Lord will come mightily upon you and you will prophesy with them, and you will feel and act like a different person. From that time on your decisions should be based on whatever seems best under the circumstances, for the Lord will guide you. Go to Gilgal and wait there seven days for me, for I will be coming to sacrifice burnt offerings and peace offerings. I will give you further instructions when I arrive."

As Saul said good-bye and started to go, God gave him a new attitude, and all of Samuel's prophecies came true that day (1 SAM. 10:5–9, TLB).

The leaders of these schools were called "fathers." They were mentors whose character and gifting helped multiply prophetic ministry among the people of God. Other leaders of prophet schools included Elijah, followed by his disciple Elisha. (See 2 Kings 2; 4:38; 6:1–7; 13:14.) These mentors were there to mature the prophets under them. They knew that it takes time to forge the necessary character and discernment.

Once I was on a panel in Sacramento, California and people were asking us questions about prophecy. One person asked "What is the difference between having a ministry of prophecy and being in the office of a prophet?" My answer: "Fifteen years."

The fact is that you can have a call to prophesy at the age of three, but it takes years to come into maturity. Just think about Samuel, serving in the temple as a young boy when he was called. It was only later as a mature man that he could perform the prophetic act of anointing Saul as king and give him God's directions.

Now, it is true that Saul himself "became one of them" (the prophet school) in an instant, but his lack of character led to his downfall later. (You can read the whole story in First Samuel 13; 19:23–24.)

PROPHETS OF THE PRESENT AGE

Looking across the great sweep of history, the present age of the Church began in about A.D. 33 on the day of Pentecost when the Holy Spirit was given to Jesus' disciples. The present age will continue until the Second Coming of Christ. Prophets and prophecy are still alive and active in the present age, despite what many cessationists would have us believe.

For example, Justin Martyr (100–165) in his *Dialogue with Trypho*, utilizes the literary device of a conversation between a Christian and a Jewish potential convert. In it, he points to the gift of prophecy as part of his evidence for the truth of the Gospel.

Irenaeus (115–202), who alongside Justin Martyr and many others was canonized as a saint, clearly states that the prophetic gifts were still in operation in his day: "For the prophetical gifts remain with us, even to the present time." He also goes on to warn against false prophets, writing, "just as there were false prophets contemporaneous with [the] holy prophets, so are there now many false teachers amongst us, of whom our Lord forewarned us to beware."[1]

The Spanish theologian, archbishop, and encyclopedist Saint Isidore of Seville (560–636) was recorded as moving in the gift of prophecy.

Not all prophets were men. German abbess, mystic, composer, writer, and visionary Hildegard of Bingin (1098–1179) described her visions in writing on wax tablets, and as she grew in stature and boldness she prophetically denounced corruption in the Church.

Anthony of Padua (1195–1231), a contemporary of St. Francis of Assisi who has been compared to the prophet Elijah, was well known for his extraordinary gifts of preaching, prophecy, and miracles. In 1231, 30,000 people attended a series of Lenten services at which his words brought about massive reconciliation and restoration, to the extent that the number of clergy was insufficient to follow up with the needs of the people.

Significantly, Thomas Aquinas, one of the most influential theologians of the early church (1225–1274) wrote, "In every period there have always been some who have the spirit of prophecy, not to set forth new teaching of the faith but to give direction to human activities."[2]

In late medieval times, Robert Fleming (1630–1694) was a minister and theologian who verified that during the reformation in Scotland, God poured out a prophetic and apostolic spirit that rivaled the outpouring of His Spirit in New Testament times.[3] He was referring to such influential voices as those of George Wishart (1513–1540), the Scottish reformer who became a mentor of John Knox (1514–1572), founder of the Presbyterian Church of Scotland, and Alexander Pedan (1626–1686), a Scottish Presbyterian Covenanter who was known as Prophet Pedan.

So it goes up to the present day. Especially in challenging times, God sends prophetic voices to guide His faithful ones. Now, after two thousand years, prophetic gifts are still in operation throughout the church—you and I are witnesses to that fact and participants in the prophetic life of the Church in the twenty-first century.

AN ESSENTIAL BUILDING BLOCK

When it comes to building up the Church, the gift of prophecy is just as important as evangelism, pastoring, apostleship, and teaching (see Eph. 2:19–22). The overriding fact is that Jesus Christ Himself is the chief cornerstone, the Rock whose presence holds the foundation together. Yes, the stone was laid by the original apostles, but that was not enough to ensure that the Church would carry out her mission. Scripture was completed by the early apostles, and they formed the foundational doctrines of the community of believers. But without generations of "sent ones," apostles coupled with prophets, teachers, pastors, and other builders, the work could not have continued. Prophetic voices are needed to inspire and build up the Church, to plow up fallow ground, to equip laborers for the harvest, to plant local churches, and to go out on the mission field as messengers. The canon of Scripture is closed. Yet current-day believers with revelatory gifts continue to speak out God's *rhema* word, subject to the written, *logos* Word.

Comprising the larger Church, each local congregation has a role to play. Some have special calls to highlight prophecy in specific ways, and they may even maintain a "school of prophets." Others are better known for their missionary outreaches, their schools of evangelism, their emphasis on healing, their pastoral training, their God-in-the-marketplace instruction. The human body is a microcosm of the Body of Christ, which would not be complete without each finger or internal organ, and most importantly the Head, the Chief Cornerstone, Jesus Christ (see Ps. 118:22; Matt. 21:42).

Today each of us is called to a ministry. (See, for example, 1 Peter 4:10–11.) While there are always going to be specially gifted individuals, part of their calling is to equip the saints to do the work of ministry. To be healthy, the Church today must embrace the fullness of these revelatory dimensions of the Holy Spirit. "Dimensions" is a key word here. As I said already, no one congregation will be able to do everything. But by putting their "specialties" together, they can make up a whole Body that is vibrant with joyful health.

We must remember one thing: Love is more important than any gift. Our identity is not in being a prophet or a pastor or a teacher but in being a child of the living God. If we lapse and misplace our identity, God will set Himself against us until we turn back to Him. While we may seem to cycle through various gifts in our lifetimes, performing many different functions and responding to various callings and just plain changes, He remains unchanged and unchanging. He is our solid rock, our Cornerstone, and what we build will topple to the ground if it is not fixed on Him.

May we live to see a reemergence of variously gifted individuals and variously graced congregations and ministries that can work together to restore the reputation of the prophetic realm to credibility and authority.

May we be able to enjoy at least a taste of the work of restoration that will occur both within the Church (to the Church) and as an outreach of the Church to the world that will come as a result of the anointed messengers of God.

LET'S PRAY

Father, we thank You for our Jewish and Christian Church history as recorded in the Old and New Testaments. We see that You have spoken consistently in times past through the voice of Your prophets. We are grateful for all of the advances that have occurred as a result of what they said and did. We honor our forerunners, those who have paved the way for us today. We want to grow in the spirit of wisdom and revelation in Christ Jesus while progressing toward the restoration of all things, which has been spoken about by the mouths of Your holy prophets for centuries. We want to take up the prophetic baton and run the race vigorously, ready to pass the baton on to those who come after us. Because of Jesus and in His name, we pray all of this. Amen.

CHAPTER 3

FOUR LEVELS OF PROPHETIC MINISTRY

The one who prophesies speaks to people for their strengthening, encouraging and comfort.

1 CORINTHIANS 14:3, NIV

Years ago, I was answering questions in a panel setting and someone asked, "Which is the best spiritual gift?"

I answered something like, "The one that is needed at the moment—that's the best spiritual gift." It could be any of the gifts of the Holy Spirit, such as healings, wisdom, word of knowledge—or prophecy. At the same time, we must remember what Paul wrote: "Desire earnestly spiritual gifts, but especially that you may prophesy" (1 Cor. 14:1).

The gift of prophecy is often the most prominent, because through it God can speak directly into a situation. Prophecy displays a great breadth of applications and expressions and, as we will explore in this chapter, what I call "levels."

I know there are different approaches to this topic, depending on a person's background. I will tell you up front that my understanding comes from my own prophetic journey. It started in the Jesus People movement of the 1970s, which planted my evangelical roots in charismatic soil. Along the way, I learned to hear God's voice through the Word of Faith movement and the discipleship movement. With many others, I rode the Third Wave Movement that started rolling in the 1980s and I was part of the birthing of the modern prophetic movement in 1988. Over the years, I became part of C. Peter Wagner's endeavors toward global apostolic and prophetic reformation. Besides Peter, the names of people I could honor along the way are too numerous to mention, but some of them include Derek Prince, John Wimber, Bob Jones, Paul Cain, John Paul Jackson, Mahesh and Bonnie Chavda, Cindy Jacobs, Bill Hamon, John Sanford, Elizabeth Alves, and others whom I will mention throughout this book.

Edification, Exhortation, and Consolation

In First Corinthians 14:3 Paul supplies three descriptive words to summarize what should be the goal of any prophecy. I started this chapter with the New International Version's wording—prophecy is for "strengthening, encouraging and comfort." Other translations use words such as "edification and exhortation and consolation."

The gift is for building people up, not for pointing an accusatory finger of judgment. However, experienced prophets, especially those who occupy a recognized office of prophet, will have the capacity and authority to both equip others as well as to speak words of correction and direction.

In this chapter, I want to take some time to differentiate four levels of prophetic gifting and authority: Level One—occasional inspirational prophecy; Level Two—consistent prophetic gifting; Level Three—proven prophetic ministry; and Level Four—the office of a prophet.

Helpful Distinctions

Throughout any discussion of prophecy, we must remember the superiority of God's living word over anything that we can come up with on our own. Even if we are highly educated and very experienced, our knowledge and wisdom will fall short. Even if we are dealing with what seems to be a straightforward and simple situation, we should hold our own reactions in check until we verify them with the Holy Spirit. God's love is so much greater than ours. His oversight is so much more complete. Why do we rely on ourselves so much when He is so much better?

This chart portrays our experience of prophetic utterances:

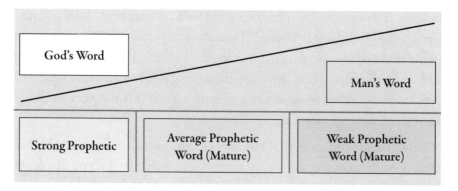

It goes along with the levels of prophetic ministry that I mentioned above:

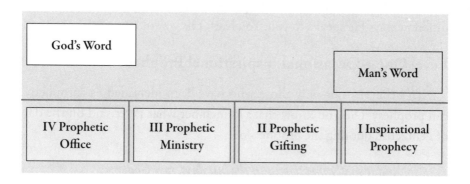

These charts are not meant to make you feel incompetent in any way. Instead, they are meant to encourage you to keep reaching for more of God's presence as you grow and mature in your use of the gift of prophecy.

It is not that inspirational prophecy or weak prophetic words that express much of the human heart are worthless—not at all. But throughout, our desire should be to be God's mouthpiece, tainted as little as possible by our pitifully inadequate comprehension. Again, as Paul put it, "Pursue love, yet desire earnestly spiritual gifts, but especially that you may prophesy" (1 Cor. 14:1).

Many of us move in and out of using various gifts and graces as our circumstances allow and require. In my case, I prophesied early on, only to become fully occupied as a pastor, caring for a congregation. I did not just sign on the dotted line to declare "I want to be a prophet." God put a desire in me, and I believe He does that for anyone He calls. He does the choosing and we do the responding. The important thing is to be faithful in whatever you are being called to do at the moment, even if it is not very thrilling. Faithfulness brings increase. (See Luke 16:10.)

By that I do not mean that you *earn* your way into a new gift or a higher level of usefulness. No, all of it is purely God's free gift. But you can *learn* how to use it capably, in the power of His Spirit and with His love, as you seek Him out every day. You can learn from your mistakes and you can learn from your victories. You can learn how to discern the voice of God in the midst of other voices. Activating all of your senses, you can find out the different ways He speaks to you. You learn His way of love.

Level One—Occasional Inspirational Prophecy

All believers, not only those who have been identified as "prophets," can prophesy. Did you know that? Remember what Peter said on the day of Pentecost, quoting the prophet Joel:

And it shall come to pass in the last days, says God,

That I will pour out of My Spirit on all flesh;

Your sons and your daughters shall prophesy,

Your young men shall see visions,

Your old men shall dream dreams.

And on My menservants and on My maidservants

I will pour out My Spirit in those days;

And they shall prophesy.

I will show wonders in heaven above

And signs in the earth beneath (ACTS 2:17–19, NKJV).

In other words, any believer is able to speak out something that God brings to mind. In addition, as I noted above, Scripture urges us to seek the gift of prophecy (see 1 Cor. 14:5).

Occasional inspirational prophecy can take the form of casual (but inspired) words of encouragement offered to other people. It can be really brief—like, "Yes." If that is what God brought to your mind to say, it is a little prophetic word. Its importance may seem slightly heightened to you, or you may know that it is something you would not normally think of saying on your own.

You just "give expression to the impression," to borrow a phrase I have heard. You notice that your heart is beating in time with God's heart of love and His fortifying comfort.

Most often these are simply concepts, thoughts, or ideas that God brings to mind, although occasionally people at this level receive visions, mental pictures, or prophetic dreams. While the potential is there to speak the very words of God, these people use their own words, primarily, to express a thought that has occurred to them.

Such words are not to be spoken from public platforms but rather are meant for a small group setting or one-on-one situation, and all parties should be willing to test them (see 1 Cor. 14:29–33).

Level Two—Consistent Prophetic Gifting

The key word here is "consistent." Prophets at this level experience a consistent stream of words, open visions, snapshot pictures, and dreams, which they are often able to report, interpret, and apply in an accurate way. Their prophetic output is still limited primarily to upbuilding words, but they are beginning to receive words with a greater weight of authority on them. Often people at this level of gifting become quite interested in and committed to intercessory prayer. This makes sense, because while prophets make the desires of God known to people, intercessors make the desires of people known to God, even as they endeavor to pray according to the will of God.

Not everyone receives prophetic words the same way. You can start to pick up how they receive words by listening to them. Some will start out with, "I feel..." or "I sense that..." while others will report, "I heard the voice of the Lord in a dream" or "I'm getting a picture of..." Others may have "open visions" (a theophany) in which they can hear the Lord's audible voice. (A theophany is sometimes an indication of a calling beyond the prophetic ministry to the office of prophet.)

Each congregational body will include a number of people who will be recognized by fellow members and leadership alike as having a prophetic gift. In time, someone with a consistent prophetic gifting could be invited to minister publicly to the congregation (again, in accordance with First Corinthians 14:29–33). This would normally happen in the context of a local congregation, which is our equipping place for ministry to the world at large. These people are gifted in that they have an unusual amount of revelation, but they must be trained not only in following the protocol of the house, but also in how to grow in maturity of character and wisdom about God's corporate purposes.

Words of direction or correction should not be spoken in a public, "unfiltered" way. They should first be submitted to the leadership in writing for possible later public delivery when it is deemed appropriate.

Prophetic people discover that their authority level increases with their track record. I had to learn a lot about that one. I could not figure out why, when I would deliver a word, nobody would even seem to hear it, but then when someone else would deliver an almost identical word, it would be well-received. It is because revelation and authority are not the same thing. Your authority level goes up as it becomes recognized by others, and that does not happen if you are forcing your way in with your gift. It depends on where and how you are serving and how much of a bridge of trust has been built over time.

Level Three—Proven Prophetic Ministry

People with a proven prophetic ministry have demonstrated over time that they possess mature character and wisdom regarding God's purposes for His people. At least occasionally, their prophetic gift will operate in tandem with "signs and wonders" gifts such as healing, miracles, or deliverance, and they will have earned the respect and authority to administer corrections and possibly rebukes. Like all words from God, theirs will need to be confirmed by witnesses and judged by other prophets, but they will be uncommonly accurate and edifying.

At the same time, they have not become fiery "thus saith the Lord" prophets. In fact, they may appear to be weak instead of powerful, speaking in brokenness and humility. (See Second Corinthians 13:7–9.) Thus, they can be misunderstood easily. Their function is to provide, in addition to significant strengthening and encouragement, sensitive direction and correction, and to help illuminate and articulate the particular truths or doctrines that the Lord wants the members of the body to know.

Level three prophets may be recognized and commissioned by their local church or apostolic network to minister not only inside the local assembly but also outside, as God leads. Often they are able to receive detailed information about those to whom they minister, including names, faces, future events, and dates. These prophets will not be strangers to open visions, and they may also deliver words in which they explain the symbolic meanings of what they are seeing. They will receive words, dreams, or visions in a spontaneous inspired flow, if not daily, at least very regularly.

Level Four—The Office of a Prophet

A person who holds the New Testament office of a prophet, although he or she will speak God's words in a powerful way, nevertheless has less authority than those who wrote Scripture (see Eph. 4:11–12). I challenge people who aspire to the office of a prophet by saying, "You are not an office ministry prophet unless you have the capacity to equip and multiply." This level of prophecy goes way beyond the scope of an inspirational gift, and they will be used most often to speak encouragement but also direction and correction, equipping and commissioning.

Distinguishing characteristics of an office ministry prophet may start at birth—a miraculous birth or an angelic visitation. The prophet may not be recognized for many years, but in retrospect this would be one of the signs. Think of the prophet Samuel, for example, born to a barren mother named Hannah who promised him to the Lord (see 1 Sam. 1). My own mother, while she was not a Hannah, miscarried a baby on July 3, 1951 and she prayed, "Lord, if You give me another son, I will dedicate him to Christ's service." And I was born exactly one year later, to the day!

Those with the office of a prophet have been proven over years of ministry, and they receive an unusually prolific flow of revelatory information. Sometimes they seem to be more at home in Heaven than on earth, especially when they report an open vision by announcing, "I was there...." Without fail, their words carry much authority, as they speak with great accuracy and power, frequently ministering in signs and wonders gifts as well. More often than other prophets, they have experienced rejection and misunderstanding. I say that they are a little bit like Jacob at times, in that they walk with a limp.

Through their gifts, they provide edification, confirmation, direction, and correction to those in church government and often to leaders in the secular world. They establish, articulate, and emphasize what the Holy Spirit wants to have highlighted. In addition, they may predict future events with accuracy to help the Body of Christ mature in its position in the world. As they are fulfilled, these predictions are used to amaze and wake up unconverted people so that they will want to encounter God for themselves.

This may include the prediction of "unspiritual" events such as weather patterns and natural signs (storms, droughts, earthquakes), international political shifts, and so on. Their accuracy gains them recognition on a broad scale, and they are used to address people of influence in the secular world as well as individuals, congregations, and streams within the Body of Christ.

I have been invited to pray and prophesy over billionaires, the chief justice of the supreme court of Korea, a NASA director, and others. I will not divulge anything about our meetings, because they are private. In addition, since I live in Nashville, I have prayed over more famous musicians than I ever would have expected.

And then there was the lady I saw in the foyer of a building not long ago. She was not famous or rich at all, but what happened was miraculous. As I started to walk out of the building, the Holy Spirit spoke to me and told me to take the money out of my billfold. I do not normally carry cash with me, but He said, "You have a hundred dollar bill in your billfold." I looked, and sure enough, I did. Then He said, "There's going to be a lady seated in the foyer as you are on your way out, and I want you to give her the hundred dollars." I saw a picture of a half-toothless woman in my mind.

I started walking and guess what? There was an old lady sitting there who was half toothless. I stopped and looked right at her and had her open her hand. I said, "Here, honey, this is for you. This is from God." I kissed her hand.

She was startled almost speechless, but she said, "Well, you mean this is for *me*?"

"Yeah, it's for you, because God wants you to know He cares. He loves you with an everlasting love. He really does." And I went on my way.

I found out she had never been to church ever in her life, not even once, but she came to church the next day. She recognized me and she said, "You're that man who gave me that hundred dollars. I never had no man touch me like you touched me." She told me that she had just been released from prison, where she had been for twenty years because she had murdered somebody. (If I had known that ahead of time, I probably would have run out the back door!)

I told her, "Darling, there's Somebody who wants to touch you, and His name is Jesus. He's going to touch you in the depths of your heart, and you will never forget it." And she gave her life to Christ Jesus on the spot.

For me, that is just as grand as prophesying to a king or a president.

THE GIFT OF PROPHECY AND THE OFFICE OF A PROPHET

Each of the four levels of activity comes from the same Lord and Spirit and they overlap in many ways. But that does not mean that we can ignore their distinctions. In fact, we must acknowledge the distinctions so as not to act presumptuously in the outworking of the gift. This becomes especially important as we consider the higher levels of operation.

Here I have listed eleven of the most important distinctions between the gift of prophecy and the office of a prophet so that we can compare them:

Gifts of the Holy Spirit	Office Gifts
• Given by Holy Spirit (1 Cor. 12; 14)	• Given by Jesus (Eph. 4)
• All can prophesy (1 Cor. 14:24, 31)	• Some prophets (Eph. 4:11; 1 Cor. 12:29)
• Edification, exhortation, comfort (1 Cor. 14:3)	• Same, plus correction, direction (Old Testament prophets)
• Given to help the Body, for the common good	• Given to lay foundation of Church, lead (1 Cor. 12:7) and equip the people (Eph. 2:20; 4:12)
• A member of the Body (1 Cor. 12:12)	• A joint of the Body (Eph. 4:16)
• Revelations of past, present (1 Cor. 12:8–10)	• Revelations of past, present, future (Acts 11:28; 21:10)
• Primarily speaks to the one body of which it is a member (1 Cor. 12:14–26)	• May speak to one body and to the nations (Acts 21:10; Jer. 1:5, 10)
• Delivers the Word (1 Cor. 14:12)	• Becomes the Word (Agabus, Isaiah, Hosea)
• Speaks to the Church (1 Cor. 14:2)	• Speaks to the past, present, and future Church, social, political, economic, geographical arenas. (Nahum, Hosea, Obadiah, Elijah, Daniel, Agabus)
• Intercessors make desires of people known to God	• Prophets make desires of God known to the people
• Speaks God's grace	• Speaks God's grace and judgment

The office of a prophet entails an increase of revelation and authority that cannot be attained apart from long experience, attentive training, and recognition (even commissioning) from others.

Keep It Simple

Our good Father extends an invitation to every one of us to learn from Him and to mature into the next level. All that is required on our part is a willing heart that hungers for more of the Lord Himself. Keep small in your own eyes and God will do exceedingly, abundantly above all that you can ever ask or think (see Eph. 3:20). Keep it simple and always let His extravagant love pour through you. Remember that the spirit of prophecy is the testimony of Jesus.

May you have the perseverance and patience to grow in the supernatural ways of God. Pray with me now:

Let's Pray

Father, in Jesus' great name we declare that we want what you want. That means that we desire to bring edification and exhortation and comfort to our part of the Body of Christ and to anybody You lead our way. We choose to lean into You, to press into Your love so that we can grow and mature in the grace that You so richly supply. Give us wisdom to properly discern and steward the present level of our gifting while we also hunger to grow and mature into a fuller stature in Your Son Jesus. Grant us increasing wisdom, revelation, and authority in every prophetic venture we undertake in the years ahead. We are truly grateful! Amen.

PART TWO

PROPHETIC DEVELOPMENT

CHAPTER 4

RECEIVING AND RELEASING THE GIFT OF PROPHECY

Pursue love, yet desire earnestly spiritual gifts, but especially that you may prophesy.

1 CORINTHIANS 14:1

As I was preparing this chapter, a picture flashed into my mind. I saw my great-grandmother Hall, my father's mother's mother. She was sitting in her rocking chair in a very poor farmhouse in rural Missouri and newspapers had been spread on the floor, because that was what we grandchildren and great-grandchildren would sit on when we had our food. I was there, and I was about three or four.

Abruptly she stopped rocking and she looked right at me and said, "You're going to be a preacher." Then and there, she prophesied. I was young when this happened, and I did not really think about it for many years.

A similar thing happened when I graduated from the eighth grade in little Cowgill, Missouri. I loved my seventh- and eighth-grade teacher, Mrs. Pickering. She was just one of those people who mean a lot to you. I was about to start high school in the next town, Braymer, which was a little bit bigger than Cowgill.

Mrs. Pickering said to me, "You're going to be valedictorian of your class when you graduate from high school."

"I'm going to be what?" I'm not sure I even knew what a valedictorian is.

"That means you will graduate at the top of your class." And then she added, "You are going to be either a lawyer or a preacher because you are so stubborn; you can argue with a fence post and win."

I guess both she and my great-grandmother were right. They did not know it at the time, but they were prophesying and I *was* called to be a preacher-prophet when I grew up.

WHAT IS THE GIFT OF PROPHECY?

Prophecy is not a learned skill, although you can learn about it. It is a gift from God that enables a person to declare the message of God to His Church for the purpose of edification. You do not have to have a good education to be a prophet. It is not an aptitude or a talent. It is an enablement, a gift, and it only operates when the Spirit has something to say. When the message is finished, it ceases to operate until the next time.

I would say that prophecy is the expressed thoughts of God spoken in a language that no person could ever articulate. The substance and the nature of prophecy exceed the limits of what the natural mind can conceive. We must never forget, "'My thoughts are not your thoughts, nor are your ways My ways,' says the Lord" (Isa. 55:8, NKJV).

The gift of prophecy comes through the *mouth of a man* but it originates in the *mind of God.* Actually, it is not limited only to coming through a mouth in words, is it? At times we hear God's prophetic word coming through instrumental music, through paintings and other kinds of art work, and through writing, including poetry; think of the Old Testament prophets such as Isaiah.

In every case, prophecy is the overflow of a heart that is filled with the Word of God. When the wind of the Spirit blows upon the *Logos*, the written Word, it becomes a *rhema*, an immediate word that can be released into many situations. *Naba* is the Hebrew root word commonly translated as the verb "prophesy," and it conveys a sense of water flowing forth as from a fountain. This is why I sometimes refer to "*naba* words" when I'm talking about prophecies.

The Greek word *propheteia* means "speaking forth the mind and counsel of God."[1] A prophecy, then, become an immediate message from God to the hearers, a divinely anointed utterance that brings life to those with ears to hear. "Prophecy is the very voice of Christ speaking in the Church."[2]

So to define prophets, you would say that prophets are those who have learned how to cultivate a "supernaturally imparted ability to hear the voice of the Holy Spirit and to speak God's counsel, not only to an assembled group of believers but also to individuals,"[3] all with the purpose of building up the hearers. Thus prophecy helps us combat, as Derek Prince put it, "two of Satan's greatest and most frequently used weapons against God's people...condemnation and discouragement."[4]

The gift of prophecy, like any other gift of the Holy Spirit, does not depend upon personality or natural gifts. In fact, sometimes it seems that God chooses someone who is weak in, for example, verbal communication or audacity, making it even clearer that prophecy is an outright gift. A person's surrender is what counts the most, not his or her personal qualifications.

Although the gift of prophecy is expressed through a human speaker, it comes from the mind of God. Paul summed it up like this:

> *But as it is written: "Eye has not seen, nor ear heard, Nor have entered into the heart of man The things which God has*

prepared for those who love Him."

But God has revealed them to us through His Spirit. For the Spirit searches all things, yes, the deep things of God. For what man knows the things of a man except the spirit of the man which is in him? Even so no one knows the things of God except the Spirit of God. Now we have received, not the spirit of the world, but the Spirit who is from God, that we might know the things that have been freely given to us by God.

These things we also speak, not in words which man's wisdom teaches but which the Holy Spirit teaches, comparing spiritual things with spiritual. But the natural man does not receive the things of the Spirit of God, for they are foolishness to him; nor can he know them, because they are spiritually discerned. But he who is spiritual judges all things, yet he himself is rightly judged by no one. For "who has known the mind of the Lord that he may instruct Him?" But we have the mind of Christ (1 COR. 2:9–16, NKJV).

PURPOSES OF THE GIFT OF PROPHECY

I want to collect together some of what I have already mentioned in order to lay out the basic purposes of the gift of prophecy. These apply to prophecy at any level:

- *Edification:* God has provided this gift to edify (build up) the Church. (See 1 Cor. 3:10–15; 14:3.)

- *Exhortation:* God wants us to earnestly incite, encourage, advise, and warn others. (See Hos. 6:1–3; 1 Cor. 14:3; 1 Tim. 4.)

- *Comfort:* Prophecy is Jesus speaking in great personal concern, tenderness, and care to release the comfort of His presence. (See 1 Cor. 14:3.)

- *To convict and convince:* This aspect of the gift can be for the sake of believers who are unlearned and uninitiated in the present-day operation of the gifts of the Holy Spirit. Prophetic messages can prick a person's conscience concerning sin and they can convey God's grace for recognition and repentance.

- *For instruction and learning:* This revelatory gift opens the Scriptures to new understanding. (See 1 Cor. 14:31.)

- *For gift impartation:* As an aspect of not neglecting the gifts of the Holy Spirit, especially prophecy, someone with the gift of prophecy can be used to impart and enliven that same gift in another believer. (See 1 Tim. 4:14–15.)

- *As a testimony of and from Jesus:* Through a prophetic message, Jesus stands in the midst of His people, telling of His works. Hearers realize that the Lord is near, not distant.

Those of us who move in the prophetic realm see God at work in a variety of settings. One day someone came up to me in a prayer line and, through prophecy, I was able to provide her some powerful and unexpected comfort. As the woman stepped forward, a strong weeping just fell on me. I had no idea who this woman was or what she needed. Inside, I felt all scrambled, and I thought, *Oh, what do I do with this? This is so sensitive.... I just don't know.* I saw a picture of someone in the great cloud of witnesses (see Heb. 12:1). I was just so torn up inside and so weepy on the outside. Eventually I just went ahead and gently shared.

"I see somebody looking in from the great cloud of witnesses, looking down upon you, and that person is smiling upon you. It could be that Heaven wants you to know something like this: You did a good job."

The woman, who had not been crying up to that point, burst into tears herself. When she could speak, she said, "I just lost a child. My son died." God had sent her a word of comfort, both about the present state of her child and about the way she had cared for him when he was still with her. That mother left the prayer line comforted.

PROPHECY IN THE NEW TESTAMENT

We can go about bringing comfort and upbuilding to others just as our brothers and sisters in the New Testament did. Here are some of the best New Testament examples of the gift of prophecy in action.

Under the power of the Holy Spirit, the priest Zacharias began to prophesy concerning the birth of his son, John. A measure of the purposes of God was revealed through this prophetic utterance, and the people were amazed:

> *All who heard them* [Zacharias's words] *kept them in mind, saying, "What then will this child turn out to be?" For the hand of the Lord was certainly with him. And his father Zacharias was filled with the Holy Spirit and prophesied, saying...* (LUKE 1:66–67).

Years later, prophecy was used by the presbytery (the prophetically gifted group of recognized elders), along with the laying on of hands, for the commissioning of Timothy's ministry as an evangelist. Paul referred to this prophetic commissioning as he exhorted Timothy to fulfill his calling:

> *This command I entrust to you, Timothy, my son, in accordance with the prophecies previously made concerning you, that by them you fight the good fight, keeping faith and a good conscience* (1 TIM. 1:18-19).

A directive word of wisdom was apparently given through prophecy to Barnabas and Saul and others while they ministered to the Lord with prayer and fasting:

> *Now there were at Antioch, in the church that was there, prophets and teachers: Barnabas, and Simeon who was called Niger, and Lucius of Cyrene and Manaen who had been brought up with Herod the tetrarch, and Saul. While they were ministering to the Lord and fasting, the Holy Spirit said, "Set apart for Me Barnabas and Saul for the work to which I have called them" (ACTS 13:1–2).*

When Paul first came to Ephesus and baptized the new believers in the name of Jesus, he also laid his hands on them so that they could receive the Holy Spirit. As we see, not only is the gift of tongues a sign of the Spirit's overflowing presence in the life of a believer, but so also is the ability to prophesy:

> *And when Paul had laid his hands upon them, the Holy Spirit came on them, and they began speaking with tongues and prophesying (ACTS 19:6).*

Prophecy and other ministries apparently combined to give Paul warnings and direction regarding his voyage to Jerusalem. This made Paul aware of the cost of his decision to make this trip:

> *And now, behold, bound in spirit, I am on my way to Jerusalem, not knowing what will happen to me there, except that the Holy Spirit solemnly testifies to me in every city, saying that bonds and afflictions await me....*
>
> *...and having found a ship crossing over to Phoenicia, we went aboard and set sail. When we came in sight of Cyprus, leaving it on the left, we kept sailing to Syria and landed at*

Tyre; for there the ship was to unload its cargo. After looking up the disciples, we stayed there seven days; and they kept telling Paul through the Spirit not to set foot in Jerusalem....

On the next day we left and came to Caesarea, and entering the house of Philip the evangelist, who was one of the seven, we stayed with him. Now this man had four virgin daughters who were prophetesses. As we were staying there for some days, a prophet named Agabus came down from Judea. And coming to us, he took Paul's belt and bound his own feet and hands, and said, "This is what the Holy Spirit says: 'In this way the Jews at Jerusalem will bind the man who owns his belt and deliver him into the hands of the Gentiles'" (ACTS 20:22–23; 21:2–4, 8–11).

In our present day, prophecy can apply in similar ways to matters great and small. It does not always need to be accompanied by religious language or even be spoken to a believer. For example, I make a point of being open to what you might call "conversational prophecy" when I reach out to people such as Uber drivers. When I call for an Uber car to take me to the airport, I pray for a divine appointment.

I ask questions and get acquainted with my driver: "How long have you been driving for Uber? What else do you do?" I like to build a bridge by talking about life callings and more. Conversationally, I can give expression to my prophetic impressions.

This may be the only way you can use your prophetic gift if your church is not open to the gifts of the Spirit. Still, it may be possible to locate a local house of prayer or small group outside of the church in which your gifts can be used more fully. There are many ministries that you can plug into that are not in competition with your local church.

WAYS PROPHECY MAY BE RECEIVED

In Scripture we can see at least four ways that the Holy Spirit speaks to and through people:

1. Spontaneous utterances: Unpremeditated impressions and thoughts (see 1 Cor. 2:9–16; 14:30).

2. Visions or trances: New Testament examples include Ananias in Damascus (see Acts 9:10–16) and Peter and Cornelius (see Acts 10–11), not to mention John's revelation on Patmos (see Rev. 1). Old Testament examples include Isaiah 6 and Numbers 24:1–9.

3. Dreams (night visions): In dreams Joseph was directed by an angel to take Mary as his wife and later to take their baby Jesus to Egypt (see Matt. 1:20–21; 2:13). Other examples of prophetic dreams in the Bible include Daniel 7:1–28, Genesis 37:5–9, Numbers 12:6, and Joel 2.

4. Angelic intervention: Angels bring God's direction to a variety of people, including the centurion Cornelius: "Cornelius the centurion, a just man, one who fears God and has a good reputation among all the nation of the Jews, was divinely instructed by a holy angel to summon you to his house, and to hear words from you" (Acts 10:22, NKJV). (See also Revelation 1:1; Acts 27:23–26.)

WAYS PROPHECY MAY BE EXPRESSED

I have been trying to make it very clear that to be considered a prophetic word, a message does *not* have to be expressed in a public venue and glorified by attaching "thus saith the Lord" to it. In fact, as you may be noticing, words from God may come forth in so many different styles of delivery that it is just not necessary to require them to be delivered in a formal way and only in a congregational setting.

Even what I call "conversational prophecy" is perfectly valid. Sometimes this graduates to prophecy in a "spirit of counsel" (see Isa. 11:2), when God's counsel can be proffered in ordinary words that are not difficult to receive. Sometimes divine words of counsel or wisdom must be written down and submitted to someone in authority. "When I prayed, the Lord seemed to be saying this...." The decision to receive the word and act on it then rests with the person(s) who received it; the prophet's obligation has been fulfilled.

Now of course there are very creative ways of expressing a prophetic message. On occasion, people may sing a word, compose a spontaneous piece of wordless instrumentation, paint a picture, or execute some other work of art, either realistic-looking or abstract.[5] Prophets have been known to act out their messages demonstratively (see 1 Sam. 15:26–28; Acts 21:10–11).

Often enough, pastors and teachers insert a *rhema* word right into their preaching. Sometimes they make it obvious that God is revealing something, and other times it is a seamless part of the preaching, almost like conversational prophecy.

Timing is as important as the mode of delivery. We all make mistakes in this regard until we learn how to discern the right place to insert what we have received from God. Do not allow yourself to feel pressured to deliver every single word on the spot. *You do not have to release everything that you receive.* Wait for the confirmation of two or three witnesses; put the word into your spiritual filing cabinet called "pending" and wait for other pieces of the puzzle to come together before you speak.

Prophetic words can be re-engaged as anointed prophetic intercession. That is essentially what Daniel did when he prayed back to God the expressions of worship and hope and judgment and great faith that he had received from God's Spirit and Jeremiah's prophetic words. Most often, you can simply pray God's prophetic blessing on someone or someplace, releasing God's grace in accordance with His will. When I can't figure out what to do with a revelation, I pray it back to God. My goal is not obtaining a platform, but rather being a good steward of whatever God has given to me. He will confirm the word if He wants me to do more with it. Or you may suddenly hear someone else delivering the same word that you are holding, as if the anointing moved over to that person, which makes you the confirming voice instead of the voice of delivery.

You do have to pay attention to the culture or environment around you. If, for example, you are not in a Christian place, you would not usually choose to stand up on a soapbox to deliver "the word of the Lord." If you are in a congregation that prefers King James English, you might just go along with that for the sake of consistency (almost like speaking the appropriate language). If they say "Brother" and "Sister," then you can, too. Assess the situation. Are you a threat, or welcome? Is the session just beginning or almost over? Your personality—and theirs—will make a natural difference. The important thing is to communicate clearly and succinctly, and to try not to go beyond the anointing or divine inspiration you have been given.

Some words are just for you. They are not meant to be shared. They are God's words to you as one friend speaking to another.

ADMINISTRATING PROPHECIES

Within each local group of believers, the leadership team has the responsibility of determining how to administer revelatory gifts. The "prophetic etiquette"[6] varies from place to place.

Small group settings are the most relaxed. Prophets can feel safer and at liberty to step out into new areas (and to learn from their mistakes). This might be a "house of prayer" or a "healing room," or it may be simply a living room full of believers who gather to study a topic or seek the Lord together.

Many churches cultivate prayer ministry teams that gather to pray for people personally at the end of a worship service. People can come to them up in the front or on the side, in the back of the room or in a separate room. Prophetically gifted people who may also be inclined to pray for healing or other types of needs can pray from the revelation they receive, inviting God to intervene in powerful ways.

Within a congregational setting, a church that welcomes the prophetic may decide to handle the delivery of prophetic words in a variety of ways:

- They may designate a "point person" or captain to whom a synopsis of potential prophetic words must be submitted before sharing (or not) as he or she indicates.

- They may set aside an approved "word gift" section of trusted, gifted men and women. This may take the form of prophetic singers who release the word of the Lord with musical accompaniment.

- They may open the microphone at certain times so that people can come forward to share, "popcorn style."

- They may require people to submit written words before or during services so that they can be judged and discerned before being read out by someone else.

Some local church leadership teams set up prophetic fellowships or peer groups. Here budding prophets can share insights, obtain confirmations, and test prophetic words. Sometimes members of such groups can be assigned to help out other outreaches and ministries, contributing a prophetic "ear" to the mix.

REASONS WHY
PROPHECY DOES NOT FLOW

The primary reason that prophecy does not flow as abundantly as it could is simple *ignorance*. The prophet Hosea wrote, "My people are destroyed for lack of knowledge" (Hos. 4:6, NKJV). Due to a lack of proper teaching, many areas of ministry may be weak or undernourished. Many environments are not conducive to prophecy, or they are openly closed to it. Unless a prophet plants him- or herself in a place where the prophetic flow is encouraged and sustained, the words will wither on the vine.

Another major block to the flow of prophecy is *fear*. This can be fear of leaders or fear of fellow members of the congregation—fear of rejection or of being misunderstood. It can be a fear of speaking out of turn or missing God or saying something wrong, even fear of expressing one's own opinion in the guise of a word from God. Or fear simply of seizing up altogether right in the midst of delivering a word in public; fear that one's faith may fail and words may not come forth. Always remember what Paul wrote to Timothy: "God has not given us a spirit of timidity, but of power and love and discipline" (2 Tim. 1:7).

Prophets must keep themselves immersed in Scripture consistently. It is not enough to read a verse or two in the morning. If the Word of Christ is not dwelling richly in a person, the Spirit has little to draw from. (See Col. 3:16.) Remember, prophecy happens when the breath of God blows on the written Word.

In addition, prophets must not neglect their prayer lives. It is by being in God's presence that we receive His word. Inconsistent prayer means inconsistent prophecy. No prayer life = no revelatory life.

Then, of course, prophets can effectively suppress the vital word of the Lord through our prideful striving for recognition. They may work hard at sounding profound, thinking that such words are more respectable than the simple ones. The Lord honors humility. If you have become entangled with a tainted belief system or movement, it may be time to confess and repent. Granted, it may take months or even years for full restoration and recovery to occur. But eventually new growth can come even out of burned-over fields.

ALWAYS LEARNING

Never stop learning and never stop waiting for God's go-ahead. I have carried many words as long as seventeen years before I felt I could release them. Occasionally I have moved to a new church or peer grouping. I let people speak into my life. I pore over the Scriptures that have to do with prophecy, as well as those that help me live a life of total commitment to God.

All of this helps me avoid certain trouble spots along the way. I have learned these practical points of wisdom:

- *Avoid prophesying your pet doctrine or emphasis.* I must yield my opinions and prejudices in order to express a pure stream of revelation.

- *Avoid condemnation.* Refrain from scolding or lecturing people through prophecy. Condemnation does not come from the Spirit of Christ (see Rom. 8:1).

- *Avoid public correction of leaders.* Honor those in authority with your words, including your prophetic words. All of us are called not to criticize (see Rom. 13:1–5; 1 Pet. 2:17), but rather to pray for leaders. Never release words that create pressure for people to perform.

- *Avoid specific personal predictions.* Use wise restraint when giving prophetic input about matters such as dating and marriages, births and deaths.

+ *Do not be a "problem-oriented person."* Speaking only from one's own knowledge of current circumstances and problem areas can create additional unnecessary problems and hopelessness. Assess problems and then pray for God's wisdom. Always prophesy life.

+ *Stay in tune with a public meeting.* Do not prophesy at cross-currents to the overall tenor and flow of a meeting. Flow with the Spirit as He is expressing Himself there. Do not introduce confusion or your own negative emotions into the mix.

+ *Stick to the Word of God.* Do not voyage too far from that shore, especially if you are a beginner.

+ *Stay within your boundaries.* Stay within your measure of faith. Do not be subject to the fear of man. Strive to please the Lord in everything. Remember the instruction: "We have different gifts, according to the grace given to each of us. If your gift is prophesying, then prophesy in accordance with your faith" (Rom. 12:6, NIV).

+ *Seek confirmation.* You are not playing a solo and you do not have to rush into it. God will speak the same thing through someone else or by another means. He will reinforce for you what He wants to say.

+ *Be governed by love.* Above and through all, let the love of Christ constrain you. Let love be your aim (see 2 Cor. 5:14; 1 Cor. 13:1–3; 14:1). Ask yourself: "Does this sound like Jesus?" "Will this build up those who hear it?"

LET GOD USE YOU

Sometimes people ask me if our own personalities get in the way of prophecy—or help. They may be concerned lest they add to the word from their own hearts and minds. Here is how I look at it: Is it not our goal to become more and more like Jesus as we grow closer to Him? Did He not make people with a variety of personalities and allow them to experience many challenges? As we mature, it is to be hoped that we will reflect Him everywhere, and that includes when we prophesy. We should not reflect our favorite prophet or the prophetic culture around us as much as we reflect Him.

So ask yourself: Did what I say or do leave the fragrance of Jesus behind? Will people remember His touch?

That old lady in Baltimore (previous chapter) will eventually forget me. She never knew my name anyway. But she will never forget the man Christ Jesus who took the time to touch somebody who had just been released from twenty years in prison. There was nobody at the prison gates to meet her, and nobody knew where to take her. So they just dropped her off on the street. Little did she know that she was about to get adopted into the family of God.

Invitations have been sent out to people like you, people who are hungry for more of God. You have been invited to take classes in the school of the Holy Spirit. Come and join me as we learn how to speak for Him wherever He may send us!

LET'S PRAY

Father, in Jesus' wonderful name we earnestly desire the spiritual gifts and especially that we might prophesy. Teach us how to receive and release the gift of prophecy, and how to walk in Your wisdom every day. We want to see a greater impact of the prophetic in our generation. Have Your will in our lives. Refine us! Cleanse us! Empower us! Open our hearts to receive more of You. Release new prophetic gifts, pure and authentic, in our generation so that we can demonstrate the love of Jesus better than ever. We want to walk in Your steps. Amen.

CHAPTER 5

Building Blocks:
The Anatomy of
a Prophetic Word

*Then the Lord came down in a pillar of cloud and stood at
the doorway of the tent, and He called Aaron and Miriam.
When they had both come forward, He said, "Hear now My
words: If there is a prophet among you, I, the Lord, shall
make Myself known to him in a vision. I shall speak with him
in a dream."*

NUMBERS 12:5–6

1988 was a significant year for the Body of Christ. The date itself carries
symbolic meaning. Eight is thought of as the number of new beginnings, and this was double-eight, doubled new beginnings.

At the time, I was in Kansas City with Mike Bickle and others, where
we became part of the birthing of the modern prophetic movement. We
had been learning a lot directly from the Bible and the Holy Spirit, but we

needed perspectives from other streams where the prophetic gift had been well cultivated. I remember learning a three-stage process that helped me and many others figure out what to do with prophetic input.

Bill Hamon (the mature prophet who is the founder of an extensive ministry called Christian International) taught us about the meaning and importance of these three basic principles, which build upon each other: (1) revelation, (2) interpretation, and (3) application. Without that framework, we would have had to learn everything the hard way. For example, we might have continued to take every word literally, never realizing that God might sometimes speak in symbolic language. Those three principles have become vital building blocks in our understanding of the gift of prophecy, to the point that we now almost take them for granted.

I do not want us to neglect them, because they are so foundational. In this chapter I will go into some detail about how to interpret and apply the revelations we receive from God.

RECEIVING PURE REVELATION

How can we know if a word is genuine? It is too easy to dismiss a word as being "off" simply because we do not consider all of the factors.

First, we must evaluate the *source* of the word. Let's say that you are learning how to use your prophetic gift and a thought crosses your mind. Simply because you are a prophet, does that mean it is from God? Not necessarily. We must learn to discern the difference between three different voices that can sometimes sound almost the same: God's Holy Spirit, our own thoughts, and satan.

John advises us to "test the spirits to see if they are from God" (1 John 4:1). How should we do that? We cannot test a word by its fruits yet, if it has not been delivered, but we can anticipate its results to some extent. Will the word express God's love to the hearers, even as it convicts them?

Or will it bring them condemnation and hopelessness? Are your own emotions and opinions part of the mix? Have you left an opening for the devil in your own life lately?

Jeremiah wrote, "I have not sent these prophets, yet they run around claiming to speak for me. I have given them no message, yet they go on prophesying" (Jer. 23:21, NLT; see also Ezek. 13:1–2). People can speak out of personal desire or ambition or a sense of urgency. We all know what it feels like to speak out of an unsanctified place in our hearts.

Just because something comes to us in a "spiritual" way does not guarantee that it comes from a pure source. Satan is a spirit, too, and he is deceptive by nature. "This is the spirit of the antichrist," wrote John (1 John 4:3). Even one of Jesus' premier disciples, Peter, had to suffer a rebuke from the Lord "Get behind Me, Satan!"—really a rebuke of the evil spirit who had incited him to say, "God forbid it, Lord! This shall never happen to You" (Matt. 16:22–23).

If you're just not sure, the wisest course of action is to either hold on to the word until you know what to do with it, or to present it with qualifications ("It seems that God might be saying something like this...").

The written Word of God is always the best test of any word of revelation. As the psalm tells us: "Your word is a lamp to my feet and a light to my path" (Ps. 119:105). In particular, a word will more likely be genuine if a prophet has been studying the Word and letting it inform his or her thoughts and judgments. A good example is the prophet Daniel, who wrote:

> *It was the first year of the reign of Darius the Mede, the son of Ahasuerus, who became king of the Babylonians. During the first year of his reign, I, Daniel, learned from reading the word of the Lord, as revealed to Jeremiah the prophet, that Jerusalem must lie desolate for seventy years* (DAN. 9:1–2, NLT).

His attention was on the message of the Word of God, and he humbled himself to know more. He meditated on the written Word for a long time.

He resisted the fearful uncertainty that the evil one sent his way. And he got it right; his prophetic words and actions brought about the fulfillment of the very Word of God.

As we have already explored, words from God do not come to us only as thoughts that are meant to be spoken. The Lord makes His words known to us in a wide range of ways, including visions, dreams, parables (see Hosea 12:10), "dark sayings" (see Ps. 78:2, Prov. 1:6), natural things (see Jer. 18), angelic encounters, and, as He did with Moses, face to face (see Num. 12:8).

The mode of revelation is not as important as the message. If God wants to get His word across, He will use the most appropriate means to do it. "Hear now My words: if there is a prophet among you, I, the Lord, shall make Myself known to him in a vision. I shall speak with him in a dream" (Num. 12:6).

Proper Interpretation

Too often, genuine words from God have been judged as false because of a misconception, wrong timing, or a misinterpretation and thus a wrong application.

As a Gentile believer, I am eternally grateful that Peter got it *right* when he was presented with the vision of the sheet filled with foods that he as a Jew was forbidden to eat (see Acts 10). Not that he found it easy to understand: "Peter was greatly perplexed in mind as to what the vision which he had seen [revelation] might be [interpretation]" (Acts 10:17). We are familiar with the story of how he decided to violate his Jewish conscience in order to explain the Gospel to the Gentile Cornelius and the others.

In his first letter, Peter made specific mention of how the earlier prophets had tried to comprehend what the Messiah would be like:

> *The prophets who prophesied of the grace that would come to you made careful searches and inquiries, seeking to know*

what person or time [interpretation] *the Spirit of Christ within them was indicating* [revelation] *as He predicted the sufferings of Christ and the glories to follow* (1 PET. 1:10–11).

Over time, their skewed interpretation that the Messiah would be more of a conquering King than a Suffering Servant made it difficult to recognize the true Messiah when He came. Some missed their day of visitation altogether. Proper interpretation is always important!

But we can never expect to understand spiritual matters; our human comprehension is inadequate. Rather than trying to understand everything on our own, it is vital to simply ask God for interpretation help. That is what Zechariah did. He said, "I saw at night [revelation]...then I said, 'My Lord, what are these?'" [In other words, "what is the interpretation?"] (Zech. 1:8–9). Though Zechariah was a seer with a proven track record, he did not assume he could interpret properly. As Bob Jones used to say to us less mature prophets, "It's the wrong time to be a know-it-all." We must cultivate seeking hearts. Daniel gives us another example: "When I, Daniel, had seen the vision [revelation]...I sought to understand it [interpretation]" (Dan. 8:15).

As he traveled from place to place, Paul and his companions had to learn how to interpret the guidance of the Holy Spirit, which came through various means and not a little trial and error: "Having been forbidden by the Holy Spirit to speak the word in Asia" (Acts 16:6) they next tried to cross into the province of Bythnia (now part of Turkey) where, once again, "the Spirit of Jesus did not permit them" (v. 7). Finally:

A vision appeared to Paul in the night: a man of Macedonia was standing and appealing to him, and saying, "Come over to Macedonia and help us." When he had seen the vision [revelation], *immediately we sought to go into Macedonia, concluding* [interpretation] *that God had called us to preach the gospel to them* (ACTS 16:9–10).

Prophetic words may seem to be quite specific, and yet they have shades of meaning and intensity. The best prophetic examples are the words "soon" and "quickly." When the Lord Jesus says repeatedly in John's Revelation, "I am coming soon" and "Behold, I am coming quickly," people thought he meant in the next month or year, or at least within their lifetimes. Guess what? It has not happened yet. The interpretation of those words has had to be adjusted.

People have produced whole books that are like dictionaries of Christian symbolic meanings. These can be very helpful, although they are not meant to be rigidly definitive. You learn interpretive skills by trial and error, by getting it wrong sometimes and by getting it right other times. God has a personal alphabet or language for each of us, and it is only through experience that we grow in our understanding of our own patterns of interpretation.

CORRECT APPLICATION

Having received a prophetic word by some means, it is far from an automatic process to interpret its meaning and assess how to deliver it or act on it.

It took Joseph many years to learn how to apply his interpretation of dreams accurately (see Gen. 37, 40, 41). At first, having learned the hard way that he should not have shared his predictive dream with his jealous older brothers, he later went on to interpret others' dreams in order to make a timely application. He should have held his tongue regarding the first dream, although he lacked the maturity to know it.

In the New Testament, the account about Paul and the prophet Agabus is instructive, because it demonstrates how this respected prophet (and those who witnessed the prophecy) were not equipped to go beyond the prophetic warnings to give Paul a good application. All of them thought, because the warnings were so consistent and dire-sounding, that Paul should cancel his plans to travel to Jerusalem (see Acts 21:10–14). In every church, the people loved him dearly, and they did not want to lose him (see also Acts 20:36–38). Some other disciples in Tyre had even told Paul directly not to go to Jerusalem (see Acts 21:4).

It was true that imprisonment and much personal harm awaited him. But Paul himself had heard from the Lord about this, and he had already made up his mind to go anyway, because he felt it was the will of the Lord:

> *See, now I go bound in the spirit to Jerusalem, not knowing the things that will happen to me there, except that the Holy Spirit testifies in every city, saying that chains and tribulations await me. But none of these things move me; nor do I count my life dear to myself, so that I may finish my race with joy, and the ministry which I received from the Lord Jesus, to testify to the gospel of the grace of God* (ACTS 20:22–24, NKJV).

What excellent discernment and tenacity and courage! Paul was not unmoved by their tears and pleas, for he respected their prophetic gifts and he knew that the consequences of his actions could be fatal. But when faced with the choice (the application of God's word) he decided, *My life is not my own. I am going to pay the cost and go to Jerusalem, regardless. I fully expect to get put in prison and more*—which is what happened.

APPROPRIATING GOD'S WORD

Sometimes we do hear the Lord, but because we respond out of our minds or with a preconceived negative understanding, we reject a word as invalid. We read in Hebrews: "The word they heard did not profit them, because it was not united by faith in those who heard" (Heb. 4:2).

Other times, the hearts of the prophets or hearers are just not "good soil," as Jesus put it in his Parable of the Sower (see Matt. 13:1–23). The parable portrays the importance of having the proper condition of heart in order to receive the implanted word of God. The same seed was sowed to all, but only some of it took root and flourished.

Can we change the condition of the soil of our hearts, making it more receptive and favorable to growth? Yes, we can. Our hearts can be watered and softened through praise and worship and forgiveness, walking in community with others.

So we see that at least three keys are needed to unlock God's prophetic words so that the proper actions can be taken. They are as follows: (1) faith, (2) the right soil, and (3) diligence in seeking.

What did Daniel do when he learned from Jeremiah's prophecy that the desolation of Jerusalem would last for seventy years? He gave himself to seeking the face of God through prayer and fasting. Such diligence in seeking is an important part of appropriating God's promises. He was tenacious, seeking God persistently even though conditions had not yet changed, and his steadfastness was rewarded.

When we have been presented with a promise from God, our diligent seeking must often include questions about the unrevealed conditions that must be met before the word can come to pass. A conditional clause lies behind each promise, and it is not always obvious.

For example, when God promised Solomon that He would heal the land and turn back the tide of punishments, he made it conditional upon the response of the people: "If my people, which are called by my name, shall humble themselves, and pray, and seek my face, and turn from their wicked ways; then will I hear from heaven, and will forgive their sin, and will heal their land" (2 Chron. 7:14, KJV). A similar condition is attached to God's word spoken through Jeremiah (see Jer. 18:8). That is also what happened when God sent Jonah to preach to Nineveh. He gave them forty days to repent—and they did. Thus he did not destroy the city and its inhabitants (see Jon. 3:4–10).

Remember how Hezekiah's tearful seeking changed the outcome of Isaiah's dire prophecy. The prediction was conditional, and only the king's earnest response could turn it around:

> *In those days Hezekiah became ill and was at the point of death. The prophet Isaiah son of Amoz went to him and said, "This is what the Lord says: Put your house in order, because you are going to die; you will not recover."*
>
> *Hezekiah turned his face to the wall and prayed to the Lord, "Remember, Lord, how I have walked before you faithfully and with wholehearted devotion and have done what is good in your eyes." And Hezekiah wept bitterly.*
>
> *Before Isaiah had left the middle court, the word of the Lord came to him: "Go back and tell Hezekiah, the ruler of my people, 'This is what the Lord, the God of your father David, says: I have heard your prayer and seen your tears; I will heal you. On the third day from now you will go up to the temple of the Lord. I will add fifteen years to your life. And I will deliver you and this city from the hand of the king of Assyria. I will defend this city for my sake and for the sake of my servant David'"* (2 KINGS 20:1–6, NIV).

HEART MOTIVATION

Truly God looks into the hearts of both those who receive prophecies and those who deliver them. He matches His words to the hearts, for His purposes, revealing the heart motivation in the process:

This is what the Sovereign Lord says: The people of Israel have set up idols in their hearts and fallen into sin, and then they go to a prophet asking for a message. So I, the Lord, will give them the kind of answer their great idolatry deserves. I will do this to capture the minds and hearts of all my people who have turned from me to worship their detestable idols (EZEK. 14:4–5, NLT).

God always looks deeply into our hearts. What is our real inner motivation? Do we want glory for the Lord or promotion for ourselves? Sometimes prophets can become overly concerned about their reputations, trying hard to be right. You can be wrong in having the goal of being right, you know. A heart motivation of developing a good track record is not the same as letting love be your aim (see 1 Cor. 14:1).

I heard C. Peter Wagner say, toward the end of his life: "You know, the older you get, the easier it is to confess that you're wrong." Most of us cling tightly to the goal of being right and find it difficult to confess our mistakes. We have to grow into letting love be our only motivation and our goal.

DISCERNING THE TIMING

There is a *kairos* time, an appointed, strategically appropriate time, for events to occur. Prophets need discernment as they deliver words concerning events and developments. Almost nothing is instantaneous. Fulfillment is a process, as Jesus said: "The soil produces crops by itself; first the blade, then the head, then the mature grain in the head" (Mark 4:28). He Himself was the fulfillment of many promises, and yet the timing of His coming was not clear until it happened: "when the fullness of the time came, God sent forth His Son" (Gal. 4:4).

Often enough, so much time elapses between the prophetic word and its fulfillment that we almost lose track of it. Think of Joseph's dream about the sheaves bowing down to him (see Gen. 37:5–8) or the long centuries of waiting for the fulfillment of prophecies about the Messiah. Habakkuk's word is a wise one: "For the vision is yet for an appointed time; but at the end it will speak, and it will not lie. Though it tarries, wait for it; because it will surely come, it will not tarry" (Hab. 2:3, NKJV).

Discernment is doubly important because of the way God speaks in parables and symbols. The Holy Spirit may speak very clearly, only to have the fulfillment surprise everyone. Here again, consider the many prophecies about the Messiah, which were almost always understood as predicting a victorious kingly figure with political power. And to add to the contradictions, when He did come, he arrived in the form of a baby.

GROWING INTO FRUITFUL PROPHETIC MATURITY

The Lord's ways are not our ways and His thoughts are not our thoughts. His ways are far above ours, and He knows the end from the beginning, unlike us. Without stifling the Holy Spirit and being over-cautious, we must nevertheless not swing the other way into ungoverned license. We must learn to hold His words loosely enough to weigh them against all of these disparate factors, trusting that He will fulfill them and keep us on track with Him.

A prophet is not prophetic every time he opens his mouth; he may be "off duty" and that may make him seem to be neglecting the unresolved words that are still circulating.

This gives all the more reason to create an atmosphere of faith and expectation so the Holy Spirit can move freely in His own timing, speaking however He decides to do.

Let's Pray

Gracious heavenly Father, we thank You for making known to us not only Your words but also Your wisdom about what to do with Your words. Our desire is to walk in pure revelation, in clearer interpretation, and in accurate application. If we are to succeed in our walk with You, we will need an abundance of Your great grace. Help us to keep our heart motivation pure so that we can discern Your timing, present Your word appropriately, and grow into fruitful prophetic maturity. We are grateful beyond words for the call You have given each one of us to present Your word to others. Our joy is in You and we pray in Jesus' holy name. Amen.

CHAPTER 6

THE PROPHET AND THE REJECTION SYNDROME

The Spirit of the Lord is upon Me, because He has anointed Me to preach the gospel to the poor; He has sent Me to heal the brokenhearted, to proclaim liberty to the captives and recovery of sight to the blind, to set at liberty those who are oppressed; to proclaim the acceptable year of the Lord.

LUKE 4:18–19, NKJV

J esus came to set you free! In the passage above, He announced to the world that He was the One who had come to fulfill Isaiah's prophecy. As we walk into His freedom, we also participate in His ongoing ministry to others, and this entails sharing in all of its inevitable ups and downs. This may come as news to you, but you and I can expect to experience our portion of His sufferings, including outright rejection.

Jesus was and is "despised and rejected—a man of sorrows, acquainted with deepest grief" (Isa. 53:3, NLT). That means that we will be, too, as we speak for Him and walk alongside Him. This is a given for all believers, perhaps even more so for prophetically gifted people. For as long as we live on earth, we can expect to be misunderstood and misrepresented, not to mention refuted, accused, and denounced. This should not come as a shock, but it does.

Still, even if we accept that wounds and differences of opinion will always occur, we do not want them to breed ungodly beliefs or lies about our value as children of God. We need to learn how to maintain a godly perspective, how to draw on His grace, how to forgive, how to lay down our lives, how to love in the face of serious opposition. We also need to be able to understand ourselves so that we can step free of oversensitivity and fear.

The Lord will never allow more pain than we can bear with His help, and He promises to deliver us after the suffering has run its course:

> For the Lord has called you, like a wife forsaken and grieved in spirit, even like a wife of one's youth when she is rejected," says your God.
>
> For a brief moment I forsook you, but with great compassion I will gather you.
>
> In an outburst of anger I hid My face from you for a moment, but with everlasting lovingkindness I will have compassion on you," says the Lord your Redeemer (ISA. 54:6–8).

SENSITIVE BY NATURE

We prophetic people come in all shapes and sizes, and our upbringing and personal experiences vary widely. But in my view, many of us tend to be more sensitive by nature, which may make us better prophets, but which also makes any form of rejection more painful.

What do I mean by rejection? Part of rejection is not feeling understood or valued and therefore being unwanted. Rejection makes you feel excluded, not part of the group, as if you are on the outside looking in. You so much want people to love you, and you are dismayed repeatedly when they do not even seem to care.

Much of the time, a sense of rejection stays hidden, although eventually it may begin to manifest itself in the form of physical ailments and emotional behaviors. As the proverb says, "The human spirit can endure in sickness, but a crushed spirit who can bear?" (Prov. 18:14, NIV).

To help us take hold of the problem of rejection, we need to examine it more fully. Our reactions to perceived rejection commonly take both internal and external forms, including the following:

+ *Loneliness.* ("I am all alone, even in a crowd. Nobody cares.")

+ *Self-pity.* ("I am miserable. Why did God make me this way?")

+ *Depression, gloominess.* ("Nothing will ever change. I will be like this the rest of my life.")

+ *Despair, hopelessness.* ("It's no good; I might as well give up.")

+ *Death wish.* ("I wish I were dead.")

+ *Suicide.* ("What's the point of living? I'm going to take my own life." [spiritual and physical death])

+ *Defensive indifference.* ("So what? Who needs them anyway? Nobody will ever hurt me again. I'm putting up an impassible barrier.")

+ *Rebellion.* ("If they are against me, I will be against them. I hate them!" [church, God, and so forth])

+ *Witchcraft.* ("I will show them!" followed by a descent into the occult, drugs, other addictions, and false gods.)

These are some of the many things that we need to be set free of by means of the saving and healing power of the Holy Spirit. Many of these all-too-human reactions can be traced to our families of origin, yet we do not have to stop with the human diagnosis, because the mercy of God can reach back in time to make everything new.

In my own family growing up, I suffered much verbal and physical abuse from my father. God made it right at the end of his life, but in the meantime I had to learn how to walk in forgiveness and how to conduct myself as a son of a perfect heavenly Father. I had to learn that I did not have to reach perfection on my own strength. I had to learn not to fear retribution. My heavenly Father loves me simply because He made me. I am His; He said my name was inscribed on the palms of His hands (see Isa. 49:15–16).[1] This is true for you, as well. God's healing touch manifested itself over time, sometimes in dramatic ways and sometimes through my concerted effort to establish His truth in my heart. I learned (and I'm still learning) how to trust Him all the way, all the time.

REJECTION: SIGNS AND CAUSES

It is accurate to say that we prophets seem to be very good at arousing rejection. Some of this would happen even if our presentation of God's word were perfect, yet we can learn from experience how to provoke less of it.

To start with, we must allow God's light to expose our hearts. Prophets, easily hurt and anticipating further negative responses, may become reclusive and withdrawn—or the opposite, defensively assertive. With feelings that are easily hurt, the prophet may see injury where none was intended; he or she may take too many remarks or criticisms personally or expect to be overlooked. The prophet may come across as grumpy, argumentative, opinionated, quick to debate a point. Or, swinging to the other side to compensate, the prophet may laugh too much, even acting giddy, or seem unable to differentiate between serious prophetic words and trivial ones. The prophet may simply talk too much without saying much that is meaningful. A prophet who feels rejected may start to act self-important. He or she may require a special invitation to participate in something, and once there may demand to be the center of attention.

In other words, anticipating rejection, prophets too often over-compensate—thus incurring still more rejection. It is not hard to see why. Other people cannot be expected to react well to someone who aggravates them, especially when it happens in a repeated way. Here are some of the ways an immature prophetic person can do this. He or she can...

...demand time, prominence, or authority.

...exaggerate gifts or embellish revelations.

...give inaccurate revelations and prophecies.

...present himself or herself inaccurately as being more mature.

...make public adversarial attacks on people (speaking *at* people instead of *with* and *to* them).

Is the problem pride, a sense of entitlement, arrogance, or the opposite? Whatever the origin of the personal behavior, it results, sooner or later, in disconnectedness from God, which swiftly renders the prophet ineffective. Projects and initiatives may go unfinished. It is almost as if the prophet's negative expectations and predictions of rejection become self-fulfilling prophecies. Obviously, these human reactions play right into the hand of the devil. He hates God and he hates God's people. He will do whatever it takes to sow strife and division.

Now to be sure, the battle is not all on the prophets' side. Pastors and leaders can provoke such reactions, often out of unresolved issues of their own. Everyone needs more of God's love and wisdom, all the time! I am sure that all of us can agree on that.

Sometimes pastors and leaders start out by overvaluing and overemphasizing prophecy. Then when they bring it down to its proper position in the church, the prophets can feel devalued and dishonored. Other times, they fail to shepherd prophets well. They may neglect to communicate success or failure, fail to encourage or correct, or forget to keep track of the results of prophetic words. At the least, this may build in a prophet an inaccurate assessment of his or her maturity, but more often it will contribute to their sense of isolation.

Some leaders will make prophets into trinkets or tokens of their own success as pastors of well-rounded five-fold-ministry churches. "Just look! We have X number of reputable prophets. We are doing so well." Others are so eager to keep up good appearances that they will actively put young prophets down, telling them that they will never make the grade. They can be guilty of devaluing the prophetic office to the point of removing prophets from roles to which they have been called by God, to the detriment of the Body. Their perfectionistic concern does not allow room for learning or growth.

Rejection, real or imagined, always involves two parties: the "rejector" and the "rejectee." Both prophets and leaders—and perhaps particular prophets who *are* leaders—need to work through their unresolved personality issues in an intentional, ongoing way, with the ever-present help of the Holy Spirit.

CURES FOR THE REJECTION SYNDROME

For the most part, the responsibility for determining and applying the cure for these patterns of rejection lies with the leaders of the Church body. They must give their prophetic people room to learn and room to fail, with appropriate pastoral feedback. Everything they do must be done in love, including confronting character weaknesses that are impinging on the clear delivery of the word of the Lord. Any discipline that proves necessary should be appropriate to the trespass and should not dishonor the integrity of the prophet. Pastoral leaders should determine to work at listening and understanding revelations *with* the prophets who receive them. It is OK to ask questions, to make assessments of progress and improvements, to consider matters of lifestyle and presentation. Leaders need to keep themselves humble, quick to apologize and repent for mishandling situations. Everyone needs to recognize that people make mistakes, but that God is always bigger than our failures.

In short, no birth is ever clean and tidy. And that includes the birthing of the prophetic in a church body. Prophets may well be quite different from non-prophets, and others, leaders in particular, may find it quite challenging to accept the "package" of the prophetic gift in their midst. But prophets do not help the situation when they project an over-developed spirituality or act as if they are intellectually superior somehow.

Another way to think of it is this: Prophets may need to repent of essentially cursing their gift by yielding to the rejection syndrome, reacting in fleshly ways to real or perceived missteps on the part of others. They must learn how to be loving and patient, even in the face of actual rejection.

Pastoral leaders are responsible for teaching the whole congregation about prophetic matters. This will not only help the word of the Lord to take root as it should, but it will prevent people from either over-exalting prophets in their midst—or turning against them and even crucifying them. Love, patience, and forgiveness all around are always in order.

Every person, whether delivering prophecies or administrating the prophetic presence in a body of believers, must remember to evaluate the ultimate fruit both of the prophetic words and of the lives of the people who deliver them. The freedom of Christ is the most important goal, not voluminous prophetic output. The freedom of Christ includes liberty from addictive patterns and unhealed emotional wounds, as well as deliverance from the influence of any evil spirits who may have attached themselves to negative patterns. Sorting such things out can be, as I mentioned, rather messy—but it is worth the effort.

The relationship between the leadership (senior pastor or team) and a prophetic minister may develop to resemble the relationship of a parent and maturing child, or that of a husband partnered with his wife. Such relationships require much attentive nurture in order to remain healthy and avoid pitfalls. It only works when all parties seek God consistently and passionately. Love must prevail!

BE PART OF A CHURCH

All the godly advice in the world does not guarantee freedom from rejection. Prophets (along with their overseers) must proceed with that risk in mind. The prophetic lifestyle should come with a warning: "Warning: Prophesying may be dangerous to your health and wellbeing."

To help them achieve and maintain maximum "prophetic health," Prophets must operate in the context of the Body of Christ here on earth; no prophet—even the ones with the most amazing giftedness—can hope to function well for very long in isolation. Some always try. They may have been shut out of their local church or muzzled in some way, so they go off and collect other wounded prophetic groupies and try to present prophetic words to anyone who will listen. (In these days of internet-enabled communication, they can more easily reach outside their geographical locality.) However, by exempting themselves from the governmental oversight of the Church, they run a big risk of running off the road. Such groups can develop extremely unhealthy cultures and can perpetrate excesses and errors, becoming even harder to set straight than they were before.

Without governmental oversight, prophets can easily fall into the trap of "everyone doing what is right in their own eyes" (see Judg. 21:25). This creates a situation in which there is no "wineskin" to receive revelation. There may be a lot of wine, but the receptacle is missing. It is the flip side of what happens in a church that lacks prophetic revelation. Then there is a wineskin all right, but very little new wine, as people become institutionalized and new life ebbs away.

As someone who has more than forty-five years of experience of functioning prophetically in church ministry settings around the world, I appeal to everyone in the Body of Christ to make every effort to function fully as part of a body with all its parts. From the head on down, all of them are necessary and none of them can operate well apart from the whole.

The prophet is meant to be a spokesperson on behalf of a superior, hearing the instruction of God and passing it on to others. The leadership of each church is accountable to God for what happens as a result of God's instruction. They govern the body under their charge by wisely stewarding designated resources and responsibilities. Under their diligent guidance, the gifts, callings, and ministries within the body are divergent by definition, but always united in their purpose, which is to serve God's purpose.

In particular, a prophet's job is to pray and seek God for His *kairos* word, submitting it to their elders, pastors, and other senior leaders for its application. When a prophet feels his input has been mishandled and that he (or she) would have handled it differently, it nevertheless remains best for him to guard his heart and to communicate his concerns, but not to agitate. This can be a real test of trust and loyalty. Not getting offended or feeling rejected can be a tall order. But the facts of the matter are clear: no prophet possesses more authority than his or her leaders, even with regard to his own words from God.

Jesus Himself came among us as a servant. He told us that the greatest among us is to be the servant of all: "He who is greatest among you, let him be as the younger, and he who governs as he who serves" (Luke 22:26, NKJV). Sometimes that may mean shedding your prophet's mantle for a while, dropping your title along with your need to be recognized, and simply serving cups of water to your brothers and sisters.

All of the ministries, offices, and gifts have been given to build up the Body of Christ. Therefore, they must function cooperatively, not in opposition to one another.[2] An individual may serve in one role more than another, but not to the exclusion of the other.

Over-categorization and simplistic stereotyping can prevent us from seeing the "whole counsel of God" (Acts 20:27, NKJV). To receive the fullness of Christ as individuals, we must be part of His Body. To grow in maturity and to bear good fruit that remains, we must cultivate a culture of honor.

For our mutual wellbeing, gifted individuals must seek out others. Teaming up with others is not only biblical, it might just save you from shipwreck! That is why I always say: *We are better together.*

ACCEPTANCE INSTEAD OF REJECTION

As a prophetic person, each of us needs to be like a rhinoceros—thick-skinned but with a big, sensitive heart. For too long I have been *thin*-skinned with a big heart. I have learned the hard way about feeling rejected because of my prophetic sensibilities and the primary lesson I have learned is that my flow of revelation will slow to a trickle if I do not get up when I have been knocked down. I have learned that I always need the main and plain truth of the Gospel more than I may think. The way of the cross leads home, and through Jesus we each have a personal place of belonging.

The truth is that Jesus was punished for our sin that we might be forgiven (see Isa. 53:9–12). He was wounded for our sicknesses that we might be healed. "By his wounds we are healed" (Isa. 53:5, NIV). He became poor for our sakes that we might have His wealth. Our Lord died that we might have His life. (Read all of Isaiah 53—the ringing declaration of the divine exchange.) We have been accepted, adopted, and cared for. God does not only tolerate us, He fully embraces and loves us (see Eph. 1:5–6; 3:14–15;

John 1:12–13). After all, He created us. He *always* has time for each and every one of us.

Accept the fact that you are fully accepted in Christ. Lay down your bitterness and forgive those who have rejected you. Instead of returning evil for evil or withdrawing to lick your wounds, sow a blessing. Search out Scriptures that reinforce the fact that you are accepted in Christ, loved with an everlasting love that does not depend upon your performance. Let the Spirit of God transform your mind. (To begin with, read Romans 12.) Part of belonging to Him is to suffer rejection along with Him, and that suffering knits us even more closely with Him:

> *So you have not received a spirit that makes you fearful slaves. Instead, you received God's Spirit when he adopted you as his own children. Now we call him, "Abba, Father." For his Spirit joins with our spirit to affirm that we are God's children. And since we are his children, we are his heirs. In fact, together with Christ we are heirs of God's glory.* **But if we are to share his glory, we must also share his suffering** (Rom. 8:15–17, NLT, EMPHASIS ADDED).

Accept yourself. Recognize that "We are His workmanship, created in Christ Jesus for good works, which God prepared beforehand so that we would walk in them" (Eph. 2:10). Did you know that it is not humility to criticize yourself? It is rebellion. We find it in the Bible: "Who are you, a human being, to talk back to God? Shall what is formed say to the one who formed it, 'Why did you make me like this?'" (Rom. 9:20, NIV).

So take yourself in hand. Repent and break off any word curses you may have pronounced on yourself. If your difficulties seem to be intractable, consider the possibility of seeking prayer for deliverance; at the least seek counsel from others concerning this issue.[3]

I believe that if we are following in His footsteps, we should expect to be *dis*honored instead of expecting to be honored. That should make every rejection an honor and a privilege instead of a cause for offense and outrage. We belong to our Master, Jesus, and He suffered utter rejection. We know because He said, "My God, My God, why have You forsaken Me?" (Matt. 27:46, NKJV). By comparison, anything we suffer is insignificant.

I do not know your journey with every step of its perils and power. I do know the pits and pinnacles of the prophetic lifestyle and I believe I have been part of helping to change the equilibrium in the Body of Christ. Fifty or sixty years ago, nobody talked about the place of prophecy in an everyday congregation; now it comes up all the time. This groundswell may still seem small compared to the number of congregations in the worldwide Body of Christ, but it appears to be growing steadily. As we lift up the Lord Jesus Christ, and honor the prophetic word, let's do our part to contribute to the health of His Church.

LET'S PRAY

Father, in the healing name of Jesus, we direct our gaze to You. We find our purpose and meaning in life, not from our gifts and callings, but from being Your sons and daughters. Help us to grow into maturity in our prophetic callings while learning how to walk and work together with others, effectively and in love. We look to You as our source of validation and we offer ourselves to be servant leaders in the Body of Christ and to any sphere of influence into which you lead us. Thank You for teaching us through the pioneers who have gone before us. In You, we live! Amen.

PART THREE

PROPHETIC DIVERSITY

SEVEN MODES OF PROPHETIC COMMUNICATION

There are different kinds of gifts, but the same Spirit distributes them. There are different kinds of service, but the same Lord. There are different kinds of working, but in all of them and in everyone it is the same God at work. Now to each one the manifestation of the Spirit is given for the common good.

1 CORINTHIANS 12:4–7, NIV

A s far as I know, airplanes are not in the Bible. School buses and bicycles are not mentioned, either. The book of Leviticus does not say anything pro or con about contact lenses or television. The term "trinity" is not found anywhere in the Bible. Neither is Sunday school.

Does that mean Sunday school is unscriptural? No. There are just some things that are not included in the Bible in so many words—although the applicable principles are.

That is the case with the seven models of prophetic communication that I will be presenting in this chapter. They have been drawn 100 percent from the Bible, although you will not find them listed anywhere in its pages. What are the seven modes of prophetic communication? As I see it, they fall into these categories: (1) prophetic oracle, (2) prophetic exhortation, (3) prophetic prayer, (4) prophetic song, (5) personal prophecy, (6) prophetic vision, and (7) prophetic action.

Let's take a look at each of them in turn.

PROPHETIC ORACLE

This first type of prophetic communication is actually one of the least common ones, the exception rather than the rule, although the word itself can be found in the Bible.[1] Perhaps "oracle" is not the easiest term to understand. What I mean is a prophetic declaration that decrees a thing into being, a proclamation. Such a prophetic word will always be accompanied by a special unction or anointing of God's presence, along with a high faith level.

We are talking about an authentic word from the one true God, transmitted to a prophet by God's Spirit—not a pagan "oracle" that is enigmatic and ambiguous and hard to understand, coming from the inspiration of unclean spirits such as the oracles of Delphi in ancient Greece. (Neither does a true prophetic oracle have anything to do with *The Matrix*'s Oracle, movie buffs!)

Most prophecy today and throughout history comes from the ongoing continuous activity of the gifts of the Holy Spirit and it carries conditions (spoken or unspoken): "If this, then that." A prophetic oracle does not carry conditions. Oracles are statements of God's authority. They bring about whatever they describe. They declare, "This is going to happen, no matter what, because God has said so. No conditions will have to be met."

Their fulfillment may take centuries, as with the ancient messianic prophecies, but it will happen without fail.

An oracle may be expressed in a variety of ways. More than we wish to admit, the various modes of delivery may derive from one's cultural or ethnic background, especially the tone of voice (shouting, for example) or the use of religious language, King James English, and special intonations and gestures.

Most of our scriptural examples of prophetic oracles come from the Old Testament prophets, Isaiah in particular. For instance, read his oracle against Moab[2]:

> *A prophecy against Moab: Ar in Moab is ruined, destroyed in a night!*
>
> *Kir in Moab is ruined, destroyed in a night!*
>
> *Dibon goes up to its temple, to its high places to weep;*
>
> *Moab wails over Nebo and Medeba.*
>
> *Every head is shaved and every beard cut off.*
>
> *In the streets they wear sackcloth; on the roofs and in the public squares they all wail, prostrate with weeping.*
>
> *Heshbon and Elealeh cry out, their voices are heard all the way to Jahaz.*
>
> *Therefore the armed men of Moab cry out, and their hearts are faint.*
>
> *My heart cries out over Moab; her fugitives flee as far as Zoar, as far as Eglath Shelishiyah.*
>
> *They go up the hill to Luhith, weeping as they go; on the road to Horonaim they lament their destruction.*
>
> *The waters of Nimrim are dried up and the grass is withered; the vegetation is gone and nothing green is left.*

So the wealth they have acquired and stored up they carry away over the Ravine of the Poplars.

Their outcry echoes along the border of Moab; their wailing reaches as far as Eglaim, their lamentation as far as Beer Elim.

The waters of Dimon are full of blood, but I will bring still more upon Dimon—a lion upon the fugitives of Moab and upon those who remain in the land (Isa. 15:1–9, NIV).

These words about the severity of God's judgment against the Moabites, Israel's enemies, were fulfilled, although it happened so long ago that the historical record is scanty. The distress in each of the cities mentioned by name was real.

Because such definitive words can be abused or misused, it is important to be extremely conscientious when releasing a prophetic oracle. It is too easy to attach God's name and authority to a word that He has not authenticated. A church can fall into the assumption that every prophetic word is an oracle from God, while most of them are really invitations or explanations.

In other words, prophets and those under whom they serve must exercise the utmost wisdom when employing this mode of prophetic expression. Prophetic oracles may appear infrequently, but they are perfectly valid. After all, the Kingdom of God is speech-activated. God spoke the world and humankind into existence, and He still speaks today regarding His Creation.

PROPHETIC EXHORTATION

Another mode of prophetic communication is prophetic exhortation. And there is more than one way to exhort. You can exhort by inspiration and you can also exhort by cattle prod. (Yes! Remember the phrase in Psalm

23:4, KJV, "Thy rod and thy staff they comfort me.") Prophetic exhortation is Spirit-inspired encouragement to come up higher. It stirs people to action, urging them on in their faith and toward a particular goal.

Along with its urgent tone, prophetic exhortation stimulates *courage* to achieve new goals. God exhorted Joshua with these words: "Be strong and very courageous. Be careful to obey all the instructions Moses gave you. Do not deviate from them, turning either to the right or to the left. Then you will be successful in everything you do" (Joshua 1:7, NLT). Judas and Silas exhorted the believers in Antioch prophetically (see Acts 15:30–35). "Then Judas and Silas, both being prophets, spoke at length to the believers, encouraging and strengthening their faith" (Acts 15:32, NLT).

In tone, prophetic exhortation can be emotional, although its expression will vary depending upon the personality of the prophet and the current cultural environment. Once I visited the Netherlands Antilles, an island chain off the coast of Venezuela. When they got together to pray and worship, there were so many cultural influences at work that I felt as if I had gone to Heaven, where people from every tribe and nation will be (see Rev. 7:9).[3] It seemed to me that the entire "cutting edge" culture of the church was an aspect of the prophetic. They sang in at least four languages: Dutch, Spanish (because of all the South American mission influence), English, and Papiamentu, their native creole tongue. The costume and dress of the worshipers matched their ethnic backgrounds and they even gestured and danced in different ways, all smoothly integrated within the same service. Similarly, prophetic exhortation can be expressed in a diversity of ways.

Isaiah provides us with many examples of prophetic exhortation such as this one:

> *Then you will say on that day, "I will give thanks to You, O Lord; for although You were angry with me, Your anger is turned away, and You comfort me. Behold, God is my salvation, I will trust and not be afraid; for the Lord God is my strength and song, and He has become my salvation."*

Therefore you will joyously draw water from the springs of salvation. And in that day you will say, "Give thanks to the Lord, call on His name. Make known His deeds among the peoples; make them remember that His name is exalted."

Praise the Lord in song, for He has done excellent things; let this be known throughout the earth. Cry aloud and shout for joy, O inhabitant of Zion, for great in your midst is the Holy One of Israel (ISA. 12:1–6).

The tone of the prophet Isaiah featured much prophetic exhortation. For more examples, see also Isaiah 19:25, Isaiah 29:22–24, Isaiah 30:18, Isaiah 35:1–10, Isaiah 40:1–31, Isaiah 41:1–4, Isaiah 42:1–9, and Isaiah 54:1–3.

PROPHETIC PRAYER

Revelatory prayer is one of the most common expressions of the prophetic spirit and is often referred to as prophetic intercession.[4] These are God-directed prayers, not preaching or exhortation. Inspired by God and directed back to Him, they make it possible for a prophet to pray effectively and according to God's will. On our own, we cannot come up with prayers that hit the mark so accurately. Since they are inspired by the Spirit of God, they express the desires of His heart back to Him. Often they express much more than the person praying could have understood about a given matter.

Prophetic prayers are recorded throughout the Bible. Paul wove some into his epistles, for example this one:

Now may the God of peace Himself sanctify you entirely; and may your spirit and soul and body be preserved complete, without blame at the coming of our Lord Jesus Christ. Faithful is He who calls you, and He also will bring it to pass (1 THESS. 5:23-24).

In the New Testament, other prophetic prayers, both long and brief, include Luke 1:67–79, Ephesians 3:16–19; Philippians 1:9–11; Colossians 1:9–12; Romans 15:5–7; Romans 15:13[5]; 1 Thessalonians 3:9–13; 2 Thessalonians 1:11–12; and 2 Thessalonians 3:1–5.

Most prophetic prayers in the Old Testament are long and eloquent. You can read samples in Ezra 9:6–15; Nehemiah 9:6–37; Isaiah 25:1–12; Isaiah 38:9–20; Isaiah 64:1–12; Jeremiah 12:1–6; and Jeremiah 20:7–18.

As with any prophetic or prayerful expression, it is not the eloquence that is important but rather the inspiration of the Holy Spirit. After all, He does not always use words; He is the one who sometimes prays "with groanings too deep for words" (Rom. 8:26).

PROPHETIC SONG

Yes, prophecy can be sung to a tune or even chanted. Such songs are spontaneously imparted and both the words and melody may come all at once in their entirety to the person, often never to be repeated again.[6] Others get written down and re-sung, sometimes for many years by many people. I believe that many of the hymns and songs that have endured over time have originated in Heaven. God opened the ear of a prophetic musician on earth so that that person could become a mouthpiece for what is being sung in Heaven. A manifestation of God's holy presence rests upon such pieces of music.

Lyrics are optional with prophetic song. Many times instrumentalists will play wordlessly under the inspiration of the Holy Spirit, invoking the very presence of the Lord and conveying healing messages to the hearts of the hearers. The singer or instrumentalist expresses the current mood and mind of God through music. These may be intercessory songs from the heart to God or prophetic songs from the Lord to His people, individually or corporately.

Among the many biblical expressions of prophetic song is the poetic song of Moses found in Deuteronomy 32:1–43.[7] Here is a portion of it:

Then Moses spoke in the hearing of all the assembly of Israel the words of this song, until they were complete: "Give ear, O heavens, and let me speak; and let the earth hear the words of my mouth. Let my teaching drop as the rain, my speech distill as the dew, as the droplets on the fresh grass and as the showers on the herb. For I proclaim the name of the Lord; ascribe greatness to our God! The Rock! His work is perfect, for all His ways are just; a God of faithfulness and without injustice, righteous and upright is He....

"Remember the days of old, consider the years of all generations. Ask your father, and he will inform you, your elders, and they will tell you. When the Most High gave the nations their inheritance, when He separated the sons of man, He set the boundaries of the peoples according to the number of the sons of Israel. For the Lord's portion is His people; Jacob is the allotment of His inheritance....

[Yet] "They sacrificed to demons who were not God, to gods whom they have not known, new gods who came lately, whom your fathers did not dread. You neglected the Rock who begot you, and forgot the God who gave you birth.... Then He said, 'I will hide My face from them, I will see what their end shall be; for they are a perverse generation, sons in whom is no faithfulness.... For a fire is kindled in My anger, ...I will heap misfortunes on them; I will use My arrows on them. They will be wasted by famine, and consumed by plague and bitter destruction; and the teeth of beasts I will send upon them, with the venom of crawling things of the dust. Outside the sword will bereave, and inside terror—both young man and virgin, the nursling with the man of gray hair.'

..."*See now that I, I am He, and there is no god besides Me; it is I who put to death and give life. I have wounded and it is I who heal, and there is no one who can deliver from My hand....*

"*Rejoice, O nations, with His people; for He will avenge the blood of His servants, and will render vengeance on His adversaries, and will atone for His land and His people.*"

Then Moses came and spoke all the words of this song in the hearing of the people (DEUT. 31:30–32:4, 7–9, 17–20, 22–25, 39, 43–44).

Singing prophets store up the written Word of God in their hearts, and it bubbles forth with the prompting of the Spirit of God. This is a golden aspect of "speaking to one another in psalms and hymns and spiritual songs, singing and making melody with your heart to the Lord" (Eph. 5:19).

PERSONAL PROPHECY

Some prophets' assignment is to speak to nations. Others' sphere of grace is to address the Body of Christ at large and movements within the Church. And many prophets are used to speak God's word to individuals. Personal prophecy is one of the most common modes of prophetic communication and that is what Paul meant when he encouraged Timothy to remember "the spiritual gift within you, which was bestowed on you through prophetic utterance with the laying on of hands by the presbytery" (1 Tim. 4:14).

Personal prophecy has three basic thrusts.

1. It edifies, exhorts, and comforts (see 1 Cor. 14:3).

2. It may release conviction (see 2 Sam. 12:1–7, Nathan to David).

3. It may provide information with specific direction, purpose, or timing (see Acts 21, Agabus and Paul).

It is usually beneficial to wait patiently when "words" come our way. We must test each one and weigh it against the written Word. Both Paul and John expressed this advice: "Do not despise prophetic utterances. But examine everything carefully" (1 Thess. 5:20–21). And "Beloved, do not believe every spirit, but test the spirits to see whether they are from God, because many false prophets have gone out into the world" (1 John 4:1).

To put it in differently: Seek the God of the word and the Word of God more than a personal word through a gifted person.[8] I love personal prophecy and I have prophesied over thousands of individuals, even as I have also transitioned into prophesying on a broader scale about movements of God on the earth. But I have learned to cling to the very Word of God and the Lord Himself, lest those words become contaminated by my flesh or, worse, the voice of the enemy.

Besides the Scriptures above, you can refer to the following for more scriptural examples of personal prophecy: Isaiah 37:21–35; Isaiah 38:1–8; Isaiah 45:1–7; Jeremiah 20:1–6; Jeremiah 21:1–14; Jeremiah 34:1–5; and Jeremiah 45:1–5.

PROPHETIC VISION

Many prophets in the Bible, particularly in the Old Testament, received prophetic revelation through dreams and visions. As early as the book of Genesis, that is how God made his covenant with Abram (Abraham):

> *After these things the word of the Lord came to Abram in a vision, saying, "Do not fear, Abram, I am a shield to you; Your reward shall be very great." Abram said, "O Lord God, what will You give me, since I am childless...?" And He took him outside and said, "Now look toward the heavens, and*

*count the stars, if you are able to count them." And He said
to him, "So shall your descendants be." Then he believed in
the Lord; and He reckoned it to him as righteousness. And
He said to him, "I am the Lord who brought you out of Ur
of the Chaldeans, to give you this land to possess it." ...Now
when the sun was going down, a deep sleep fell upon Abram;
and behold, terror and great darkness fell upon him. God
said to Abram, "Know for certain that your descendants will
be strangers in a land that is not theirs, where they will be
enslaved and oppressed four hundred years. But I will also
judge the nation whom they will serve, and afterward they
will come out with many possessions. As for you, you shall go to
your fathers in peace; you will be buried at a good old age...."
It came about when the sun had set, that it was very dark,
and behold, there appeared a smoking oven and a flaming
torch which passed between these pieces. On that day the Lord
made a covenant with Abram, saying, "To your descendants
I have given this land, from the river of Egypt as far as the
great river, the river Euphrates" (GEN. 15:1-2, 5-7, 12-15,
17-18).*

When the Lord God rebuked Miriam and Aaron for dishonoring
Moses, He differentiated Moses from all other prophets (which would
include prophets like you and me), with whom His ordinary way of communicating involves visions and dreams:

*Hear now My words: If there is a prophet among you, I, the
Lord, shall make Myself known to him in a vision. I shall
speak with him in a dream.*

*Not so, with My servant Moses, he is faithful in all My
household; with him I speak mouth to mouth, even openly,
and not in dark sayings, and he beholds the form of the Lord*
(NUM. 12:6-8).

THE SEER

You will notice that the term "seer" is applied to many of the Old Testament prophets. For example: "Saul approached Samuel in the gate and said, 'Please tell me where the seer's house is.' Samuel answered Saul and said, 'I am the seer'" (1 Sam. 9:18–19). "When David arose in the morning, the word of the Lord came to the prophet Gad, David's seer, saying..." (2 Sam. 24:11). "Now the acts of Rehoboam, from first to last, are they not written in the records of Shemaiah the prophet and of Iddo the seer, according to genealogical enrollment?" (2 Chron. 12:15).

Notice the differentiation between "Shemaiah the prophet" and "Iddo the seer." Seers *see*; they operate in a visionary way. *Nabi* prophets perceive the word of the Lord as it bubbles up within their spirits and minds. Seers do not typically repeat phrases, but rather describe pictures that they are seeing.[9] Their messages can change the course of history.[10]

Visions are the common language of Heaven, and any of us can expect to hear from God this way. Remember the words of the prophet Joel:

> *It will come about after this that I will pour out My Spirit on all mankind; and your sons and daughters will prophesy, your old men will dream dreams, your young men will see visions. Even on the male and female servants I will pour out My Spirit in those days* (JOEL 2:28–29).

PROPHETIC ACTION

From time to time, prophets will be moved upon to demonstrate their words physically, to act out a story or parable. The mode of communication becomes gestures and actions. Although this form of delivering a message can be radical, prophetic action should never be promoted as higher or more significant than other modes of prophetic delivery.

I'm sure you can think of some of the bizarre behaviors of Old Testament prophets. Do you remember Ezekiel shaving his head with a sword (see Ezek. 5:1–17)? How about Hosea marrying a prostitute (see Hosea 1–3) or Isaiah going naked for three years (see Isa. 20)?

Only a little less shocking are incidents such as Jeremiah and the yoke (see Jer. 27–28) or Agabus and the belt (see Acts 21: 9–14). They acted out the word of the Lord.[11] You may also remember the time the prophet Ezekiel was told to portray the upcoming exile of the people of Israel:

> *The word of the Lord came to me: "Son of man, you are living among a rebellious people. They have eyes to see but do not see and ears to hear but do not hear, for they are a rebellious people. Therefore, son of man, pack your belongings for exile and in the daytime, as they watch, set out and go from where you are to another place. Perhaps they will understand, though they are a rebellious people. During the daytime, while they watch, bring out your belongings packed for exile. Then in the evening, while they are watching, go out like those who go into exile. While they watch, dig through the wall and take your belongings out through it. Put them on your shoulder as they are watching and carry them out at dusk. Cover your face so that you cannot see the land, for I have made you a sign to the Israelites."*
>
> *So I did as I was commanded....*
>
> *"Son of man, did not the Israelites, that rebellious people, ask you, 'What are you doing?' Say to them, 'This is what the Sovereign Lord says: This prophecy concerns the prince in Jerusalem and all the Israelites who are there.' Say to them, 'I am a sign to you.' As I have done, so it will be done to them. They will go into exile as captives."*
>
> *"...Son of man, tremble as you eat your food, and shudder in fear as you drink your water. Say to the people of the land:*

'This is what the Sovereign Lord says about those living in Jerusalem and in the land of Israel: They will eat their food in anxiety and drink their water in despair, for their land will be stripped of everything in it because of the violence of all who live there. The inhabited towns will be laid waste and the land will be desolate. Then you will know that I am the Lord'" (EZEK. 12: 1–7, 9–11, 18–20, NIV).

I am not sure how quick I would be to obey a command to act out a prophetic word on the level of many of these prophets of old, although I have performed prophetic acts to accompany intercessory prayers or words of declaration, such as driving stakes into the ground and waving banners from hilltops and many other demonstrative expressions.[12]

Suffice it to say that prophetic actions are a legitimate—albeit unusual and infrequent—method for God to use when He wants to communicate in a graphic and memorable way.

CALLED TO ACTION

Despite the fact that probably none of us are likely to be called, as Isaiah was, to risk arrest for indecent exposure by prophesying naked, all prophetic people are called to action. "The people that do know their God shall be strong, and do exploits" (Dan. 11:32, KJV). There is such a diversity of expression in both the way revelation is received and the way it is imparted to others.

We take action every time we obey the Holy Spirit and express a message from Heaven. We choose the method of expression in obedience, as well. Whether we speak or write or sing or act out or pray under prophetic inspiration, we follow through, looking to Jesus who is always our shepherd and guide.

LET'S PRAY

Father, in the name of Jesus, whose name is the mightiest of all names, we hunger to experience more prophetic diversity than we have ever before. Take the lid off of our thinking and expand our hearts to receive more of Your revelation and understanding and to know how to share it with others. You are the Creator and we want to see You make something new in our lives. We do not want to be limited to one model of prophetic expression, but rather to become clay in Your hands, able to follow Your creative impulses. We want to see many pure and authentic manifestations of Your prophetic ways here and now. For Jesus Christ's sake and because of His love, we say Amen!

CHAPTER 8

PROPHETIC WOMEN

"In the last days," God says, "I will pour out my Spirit upon all people. Your sons and daughters will prophesy. Your young men will see visions, and your old men will dream dreams. In those days I will pour out my Spirit even on my servants— men and women alike—and they will prophesy."

ACTS 2:17–18, NLT

Did you know that 60 percent of the membership of the Body of Christ is women? The percentage of women is even larger—about 80 percent—when you talk about the part of the Church that is devoted to intercessory prayer. Some of the greatest "generals" in the army of God are anointed, prophetic women. They know how to pray and fast, and they embrace sacrificial living. Over the centuries, I feel that their contributions to the well-being of God's people are absolutely heroic. I wonder why any man should take it upon himself to wire shut the mouths of these nurturing, consecrated servants of God.

Women have been faithful champions over the centuries, for the whole history of the people of God. We do not know about as many of them as we could, because the (largely male) history-writers have ignored or minimized their accomplishments. Yet we do know about quite a few of them, and they represent all the different streams of prophetic expression.

Naturally, another reason that we do not know about all of the great prophetic women of the past is that many of them were restricted from taking leadership, especially leadership over men. To some extent, this is still the case, which makes women's accomplishments all the more notable. But in recent decades, even organizations that were founded by women to minister exclusively to women have decided to open their ranks to men. Thus Women's Aglow, founded over fifty years ago, has now become Aglow International (and I am one of its advisors). And End-Time Handmaidens, founded by Gwen Shaw, has changed its name and membership to include men; now it is called End-Time Handmaidens and Servants, International.

The topic of women's roles in the Church is near and dear to my heart ever since I went through a big paradigm shift. I used to be one of "those" males who believed that a woman's place was not anywhere near the pulpit. When my wife started to minister with me, she wore a head covering. That was (and is) well and good at times, but I found that I had to repent publicly to women for the way I had shut the door on them. Now I have confessed my own shortcomings along with the generational sins of the men who came before me; I have knelt in public meetings to ask women to forgive men for controlling them. I have asked women to forgive spiritual leaders for oppression and for abuse. I have never wanted it to become an emotional display, but it has always been powerful.

I remember one time at one of the global women leaders' conferences where I had a long line of women waiting to stand in front of me. They were not there for prayer ministry and they did not want me to prophesy over them. They were there so I could address the unresolved male-female injustices. One by one, I humbly asked each woman to forgive me as a representative of any man who may have used his authority inappropriately over her. Do you know what almost every one of them replied, some with tears in their eyes? "You are the first man who has ever apologized to me in my lifetime."

That is just not right, is it? I hope it will not remain the only time in their lives that something like that happens. We are all supposed to humble ourselves under the mighty hand of God (see 1 Pet. 5:6). We do not have to become shrill women's libbers to make a difference. By building a culture within the Church of honor and relational authority we can esteem one another across traditional dividing lines because, in Christ, there is no male or female (see Gal. 3:28). The simple fact of the matter is that, in giving His gifts, God does not discriminate because of gender.

Keeping in mind all that we have been learning in the previous chapters about the diversities of prophetic "flavor" within the Kingdom of God, and with Jewish and Church history as our guide, we will now take a look into the wonderful and sometimes controversial subject of women in the prophetic life of the Church.

WOMEN CALLED PROPHETESSES IN SCRIPTURE

Of necessity, this will have to be a quick overview, although whole books could be (and in some cases, have been) written about these individual women. Let's start back at the Exodus with *Miriam*, sister of Moses and Aaron. She was known as a spokesperson for God particularly as a leader in music and dance:

> *Miriam the prophetess, Aaron's sister, took the timbrel in her hand, and all the women went out after her with timbrels and with dancing. Miriam answered them,*
>
> *"Sing to the Lord, for He is highly exalted;*
>
> *The horse and his rider He has hurled into the sea"* (EXOD. 15:20–21).[1]

Moving on through the years, we find *Deborah*, who is mentioned in an unapologetic way as one of the judges of Israel. As a prophetess and judge, she stood before God on behalf of Israel and she was an advisor to the military leader Barak. "Now Deborah, a prophetess, the wife of Lappidoth, was judging Israel at that time. He used to sit under the palm tree of Deborah between Ramah and Bethel in the hill country of Ephraim; and the sons of Israel came up to her for judgment" (Judg. 4:4–5). Eventually, because of Deborah's leadership acumen, she was called a "mother in Israel" (see Judg. 5:7).

Huldah was another early prophetess in Israel. This prophetess and keeper of the wardrobe sought the prophetic word of the Lord on behalf of the young King Josiah (see 2 Kings 22:14). There were other prophets (male) in Israel at the time, but King Josiah sought her out because of her seasoned and influential ministry as a prophetess.

Then we have the unnamed woman who was *Isaiah's wife*. Almost nothing was recorded about her, as Isaiah mentioned her only once: "And I went to the prophetess, and she conceived and bore a son" (Isa. 8:3, NKJV). Some scholars have said that she was called "the prophetess" only because she was Mrs. Isaiah, but others argue that nowhere else in the entire Old Testament is the wife of a prophet called a prophetess. I have come to believe that Isaiah and his wife operated as a prophetic team!

We must not neglect *Elizabeth*, mother of John the Baptist and cousin of *Mary*, the mother of our Lord Jesus. Both of these devout women were active in prayer, worship, and faithful waiting on the Lord for the fulfillment of His prophetic promises. The interchange between these God-fearing women resulted in exuberant praises and prophesying concerning the destiny of Mary's Child, the Messiah Jesus. Here is how their magnificent prophetic exchange unfolded:

> *Now Mary arose in those days and went into the hill country*
> *with haste, to a city of Judah, and entered the house of*
> *Zacharias and greeted Elizabeth. And it happened, when*

Elizabeth heard the greeting of Mary, that the babe leaped in her womb; and Elizabeth was filled with the Holy Spirit. Then she spoke out with a loud voice and said, "Blessed are you among women, and blessed is the fruit of your womb! But why is this granted to me, that the mother of my Lord should come to me? For indeed, as soon as the voice of your greeting sounded in my ears, the babe leaped in my womb for joy. Blessed is she who believed, for there will be a fulfillment of those things which were told her from the Lord."

And Mary said: "My soul magnifies the Lord, and my spirit has rejoiced in God my Savior. For He has regarded the lowly state of His maidservant; for behold, henceforth all generations will call me blessed. For He who is mighty has done great things for me, and holy is His name. And His mercy is on those who fear Him from generation to generation. He has shown strength with His arm; he has scattered the proud in the imagination of their hearts. He has put down the mighty from their thrones, and exalted the lowly. He has filled the hungry with good things, and the rich He has sent away empty. He has helped His servant Israel, in remembrance of His mercy, as He spoke to our fathers, to Abraham and to his seed forever" (Luke 1:39–55, NKJV).

I am so grateful that Luke made a point of recording the whole thing for the benefit of generations to come. Luke seems to pay attention to details about prophetic women. In addition to these prophetic songs of Elizabeth and Mary in the first chapter of Luke, we also see mention of "a prophetess Anna" in the second chapter:

And there was a prophetess, Anna the daughter of Phanuel, of the tribe of Asher. She was advanced in years and had lived with her husband seven years after her marriage, and then as a widow to the age of eighty-four. She never left the temple, serving night and day with fastings and prayers (LUKE 2:36–37).

She was one of those devout women who chose to spend every day of her widowhood within the Temple precincts. Simeon, who had just fulfilled his lifelong dream of seeing the Messiah with his own eyes and had prophesied over him, was there, too. Mary and Joseph were aware that their eight-day-old son was special to God but Simeon's word had amazed them (see Luke 2:27–33). Prophetically, Simeon had just expressed his joy at seeing the son of God in the flesh. Then, "She [Anna] came along just as Simeon was talking with Mary and Joseph, and she began praising God. She talked about the child to everyone who had been waiting expectantly for God to rescue Jerusalem" (Luke 2:38, NLT). In other words, as soon as Anna saw the newborn baby in his mother's arms, she took it a step further, telling others that she had found the Messiah.

But why did Luke call *Anna* "a prophetess"? We have no record of any other prophetic activity on her part. That is, we have no record of her delivering prophetic "words" in public. What she did do was to pursue God with all her heart, so it became easy for her to recognize His handiwork when she saw it. She was a woman of the "secret place," without any public ministry at all except to intercede in the Temple, where nobody would notice her except the other worshipers.

In other words, Anna's prophetic ministry was expressed through intercession. Somehow she had come to know about all of the prophetic promises concerning the Messiah, promises that had not yet been fulfilled. She was on the lookout for this promised Messiah, the Deliverer and hope of Israel. Like Simeon a moment before, Anna's spirit leapt within her when she saw the little bundle in Mary's arms. This was the One! She blessed Him, knowing that all of the words of the prophets were coming to pass. I love Anna, and I know that women who are prophetic intercessors love her even more.

Jesus grew up and embarked on His public ministry (consistently honoring women, by the way), and ended up dying on the cross and rising from the dead. Within just a few decades, He had fulfilled more of the ancient prophetic words than seemed possible and He had left behind a growing Church. This is when more capable women such as Priscilla and *Phillip's four daughters* come along. Phillip, known to us as "the Evangelist," had "four virgin daughters who were prophetesses" (Acts 21:9). Apparently all four of Phillip's unmarried daughters had been acknowledged by the local body of believers as having prophetic gifts. We do not know any words or actions specifically attributed to them, but surely the term "prophetesses" must have been well-deserved.

WOMEN IN SCRIPTURE WHO PLAYED IMPORTANT PROPHETIC ROLES

Now we move on to consider the relatively large number of women throughout the Old and New Testaments who were not called prophetesses, but who played important roles in prophetic events. Their example of godly obedience should encourage us as many of us follow in their footsteps, "doing exploits" (see Dan. 11:32) that are at times so hidden that nobody finds out about them.

The only reason we know about these women is because someone told their stories in Scripture. The prophetess/judge Deborah had told the army commander Barak that he should march against the forces of Sisera, their enemy—specifically saying that he (Barak) would prevail. What she did not say was how this prophetic word would be fulfilled. (The complete story is told in the fourth chapter of the book of Judges.) Barak marched and he did prevail in battle, but the commander Sisera fled on foot and escaped. He happened to take refuge in the tent that belonged to a women named *Jael*, who rose to the occasion. Jael was shrewd and brave. She welcomed the fugitive into her domain and gave him milk to drink. At her invitation, he lay down and fell into an exhausted sleep. Then:

> *Jael, Heber's wife, took a tent peg and seized a hammer in her hand, and went secretly to him and drove the peg into his temple, and it went through into the ground; for he was sound asleep and exhausted. So he died. And behold, as Barak pursued Sisera, Jael came out to meet him and said to him, "Come, and I will show you the man whom you are seeking." And he entered with her, and behold Sisera was lying dead with the tent peg in his temple* (Judg. 4:21–22).

Jael did her valiant part to serve the purposes of God as prophesied by Deborah.

In a later time, we learn from the scriptural account that a woman named *Abigail* behaved wisely and graciously in the face of an unfortunate conflict that had deadly potential (see 1 Sam. 25). Her wealthy, "harsh and evil" husband Nabal (who, as she said herself, was "a worthless man") rebuffed the generous assistance of David's men to his men. David, still on the run from King Saul, took offense in turn. Things could have escalated badly. But Abigail intervened, presenting gifts to David and his men and praising him, while apologizing for her husband's actions. Disaster was averted. Within a short time, Nabal died, whereupon David claimed Abigail as his wife.

Such courageous women put most of the men around them to shame, don't they? Another such woman was so heroic that an entire book of the Bible is devoted to her: Queen *Esther*. If you have never read the entire book, you can do so at one sitting—the story is a real cliff-hanger. In brief, Esther, a Jewish woman in the harem of the Persian king Ahasuerus (also known as Xerxes) in the capital city of Susa, caught wind of a nefarious plot against her fellow Jews. She had kept her own Jewish identity a secret. A nobleman named Haman found an excuse to promote a decree that every one of the Jewish people would be slaughtered, across the land. Tipped off by her guardian and cousin Mordecai, who told her, "who knows whether you have not attained royalty for such a time as this?" (Esther 4:14), Esther insightfully deployed a plan to thwart the genocide. After fasting for three days, she invited the king and Haman to a series of two banquets, and at the second one she revealed what Haman planned to do. He was hanged on the gallows that Haman had erected prematurely for Mordecai and the Jewish population was spared, not only within Susa, but across all one hundred and twenty-seven of King Ahasuerus' provinces. By her prayer, fasting, courage, and prophetic insight, godly Queen Esther had saved the entire Jewish race.

Before we finish the Old Testament, we would not want to miss the nameless *Proverbs 31 woman*, who was prophetic in both her insight and her lifestyle:

> *An excellent wife, who can find? For her worth is far above jewels.*
>
> *The heart of her husband trusts in her, and he will have no lack of gain.*
>
> *She does him good and not evil all the days of her life.*
>
> *She looks for wool and flax and works with her hands in delight.*
>
> *She is like merchant ships; she brings her food from afar.*
>
> *She rises also while it is still night and gives food to her household and portions to her maidens.*
>
> *She considers a field and buys it; from her earnings she plants a vineyard.*
>
> *She girds herself with strength and makes her arms strong.*
>
> *She senses that her gain is good; her lamp does not go out at night.*

She stretches out her hands to the distaff, and her hands grasp the spindle.

She extends her hand to the poor, and she stretches out her hands to the needy.

She is not afraid of the snow for her household, for all her household are clothed with scarlet.

She makes coverings for herself; her clothing is fine linen and purple.

Her husband is known in the gates, when he sits among the elders of the land.

She makes linen garments and sells them, and supplies belts to the tradesmen.

Strength and dignity are her clothing, and she smiles at the future.

She opens her mouth in wisdom, and the teaching of kindness is on her tongue.

She looks well to the ways of her household, and does not eat the bread of idleness.

Her children rise up and bless her; her husband also, and he praises her, saying: "Many daughters have done nobly, but you excel them all."

Charm is deceitful and beauty is vain, but a woman who fears the Lord, she shall be praised.

Give her the product of her hands, and let her works praise her in the gates (PROV. 31:10–31).

By presenting such a sweeping composite of admirable qualities, the term "Proverbs 31 Woman" signifies all of the best that a woman has to offer in any culture or period of history.

Moving on into the New Testament, we find even more women who display aspects of the prophetic gift, whether or not they themselves were aware of it. For example, take the Samaritan *woman at the well,* whose name is lost to history (see John 4:7–29). Jesus singled her out prophetically, and she is considered by many to be the first true evangelist in the Bible. When she told the townspeople the good news about the Christ, many of them believed.

Sometimes I think that God plays favorites, and *Mary Magdalene* and *"the other Mary"* were surely among them. Those two women arrived first at the empty tomb, were the first to hear the words, "He is risen," and the first to announce His resurrection (see Matt. 28:1–10). Their unwavering loyalty and faith put them in the forefront of prophetic fulfillment.

Then there is *Lydia,* the well-to-do businesswoman from the city of Thyatira in modern-day Turkey whose conversion outside the Macedonian city of Philippi and subsequent outreach opened the door to the Gospel of the Kingdom throughout Europe (see Acts 16:14–15). She is considered the first convert in Europe, since she lived and worked far to the west and north of the rest of the Middle East and Asia.

Priscilla and Aquila are mentioned in several places in the book of Acts and also in Paul's letters to the Romans, the Corinthians, and to Timothy. Like Paul, they worked as tentmakers, but they were also a husband-and-wife team in another way, evidently explaining the Gospel message with exceptional clarity, moving from Rome to Corinth to Ephesus and elsewhere as the Spirit of God led them.

> *Paul left Athens and went to Corinth. There he met a Jew named Aquila, a native of Pontus, who had recently come from Italy with his wife Priscilla, because Claudius had ordered all Jews to leave Rome. Paul went to see them, and because he was a tentmaker as they were, he stayed and worked with them.... Paul stayed on in Corinth for some time. Then he left the brothers and sisters and sailed for Syria, accompanied by Priscilla and Aquila. They arrived at Ephesus, where Paul*

left Priscilla and Aquila.... Meanwhile a Jew named Apollos, a native of Alexandria, came to Ephesus. He was a learned man, with a thorough knowledge of the Scriptures. He had been instructed in the way of the Lord, and he spoke with great fervor and taught about Jesus accurately, though he knew only the baptism of John. He began to speak boldly in the synagogue. When Priscilla and Aquila heard him, they invited him to their home and explained to him the way of God more adequately (ACTS 18:1–3, 18–19, 24–26, NIV).

Greet Priscilla and Aquila, my co-workers in Christ Jesus. They risked their lives for me. Not only I but all the churches of the Gentiles are grateful to them (ROM. 16:3–4, NIV).

The churches in the province of Asia send you greetings. Aquila and Priscilla greet you warmly in the Lord, and so does the church that meets at their house (1 COR. 16:19, NIV).

Greet Priscilla and Aquila and the household of Onesiphorus (2 TIM. 4:19, NIV).

Some commentators note the fact that Priscilla's name is almost always mentioned first which was as unusual then as it is now. This may indicate that she was the most engaging teacher of the pair, the one who brought the Word to life as not many other men or women could do.

Phoebe, an early deaconess in the growing church at Cenchrea, was well known for her servant's heart and her works of mercy (see Rom. 16:1). *Chloe* hosted a church in her home (see 1 Cor. 1:11). It is difficult to tell if she was simply the homeowner-hostess or actually the pastor of the house church.

The listing of the name *Junia*—or Junias, as some translators prefer—in Romans 16:7 has caused a lot of controversy over the years. Was this person male or female? If female, was she actually considered an apostle, with all the implications raised by such an unusual role, or was she possibly married to Andronicus, the name listed right before hers, and thus serving alongside him as Priscilla and Aquila did together?

My point in cataloging so many of the women in the Bible is not to declare that all of them were prophetic in the narrowest definition of the term, but rather to highlight the idea that women have always been gifted to serve God's people in the same ways as men.

PROMINENT WOMEN IN CHURCH HISTORY

Throughout the history of the church we know of many women of vibrant faith whose gifts and courage made a difference for the Kingdom in many nations of the earth. You may recognize many of these names; they are some of my favorites: Vibia Perpetua (A.D. 181–203), Joan of Arc (1412–1431); Madame Jeanne Guyon (1648–1717), Susanna Wesley (1669–1742), Catherine Booth (1829–1890), Fanny Crosby (1820–1915), Maria Wood-worth-Etter (1844–1924), Aimee Semple McPherson (1890–1944), Amy Carmichael (1867–1951), Lydia Prince (1890–1975), Mother (now Saint) Teresa of Calcutta (1910–1997), and Basilea Schlink (1904–2001).

If you want examples of prophetic trances (being caught up into a state of ecstasy with prophetic revelation) look no further than the life of *St. Teresa of Avila* (1515–1582), who revived the Carmelite order of nuns and wrote about her experiences (her books include *The Interior Castle*, for example), to the lasting benefit of generations of believers.

In modern times, healing evangelist *Kathryn Kuhlman* (1907–1976) exercised prophetic gifts and words of knowledge along with gifts of healing and more in her public healing crusades in the United States.

At one of the national apostolic, prophetic roundtables I met Gwen Shaw (1924–2013), whom I mentioned earlier in this chapter as the founder of End-Time Handmaidens (now End-Time Handmaidens and Servants, International). She continued her many accomplishments, guided by God's prophetic light and sustained by His Spirit, well into her old age.

Today, still prophesying and interpreting dreams and praying as the Spirit directs are many women, including Jane Hamon, daughter-in-law of Bill Hamon, and also Sharon Stone of England. I am leaving many out in this quick fly-by, but how could I forget to call attention to my friends Bonnie Chavda, prophetess wife of Mahesh Chavda, and Cindy Jacobs, founder of Generals International (and one of the leading prophetic and prayer voices internationally in modern times, male or female). Among her many books is one titled *Possessing the Gates of the Enemy*, which is about prophetic intercession. Another one of the women who has impacted my life in a special way is Elizabeth (Beth) Alves, whom I refer to as the "Grandma of the Prayer Shield." Coming out of obscure beginnings, she has ministered prophetically to many kings and other world leaders in her lifetime.

In their diverse ways, prophetic leaders are often forerunners who carry a breaker anointing into the various seven cultural mountains of influence (see the next chapter). This is especially true concerning my dear friend in ministry, adventuresome and articulate media entrepreneur Patricia King of XP Ministries. When you add in the mix a woman such as the ecstatic prophetess Stacey Campbell of Canada you begin to appreciate the immense diversity in giftedness among female prophets today. They are so different and yet each is so effective in their distinct fields of endeavor.

FROM BETTY CROCKER HOMEMAKER TO PROPHETIC LIONESS

God changed my late wife, Michal Ann, from being a devoted wife and mother of four to being a dynamic, compassionate, prophetic leader and an example for other women. For many years, her dearest wish had been to be a stay-at-home mother and housewife, and she was an excellent one. Then

God gave her a spectacular series of angelic visitations that occurred night after night from midnight until five in the morning—for nine straight weeks. She was never the same after that.

She was still a great wife and mother, but she stepped out beyond her former timidity to speak in front of large groups and to lead the way in new endeavors.

My dear Annie never wavered in her heart's desire to love God with all her heart, soul, and strength, and to love her neighbor. God gave her the courage and energy she needed to reach out far beyond her old dreams; in fact, because of her books and the ministries she founded such as Compassion Acts, she is still reaching out today.

Before she graduated to Heaven, Michal Ann wrote up a brief commentary she titled, "Cultivate Your Unique Prophetic Expression." Let her words encourage you today:

> We must quit comparing ourselves to one another and quit using someone else's measuring stick on ourselves. Our eyes must be focused on Jesus and our goal must be to do and be whatever brings Him pleasure. We are each planted in a garden in the midst of a great variety of flowers. Each has its own color, fragrance, and season of blooming. Our individual lives, when lived to the fullest, release their own unique aromas to the Lord. This collective blend of individual fragrances woos and draws the Spirit's presence to walk among us.
>
> Whether you are a man or woman is really not the main issue. Are you being the unique vessel God has created you to be? Step out of your self-made limitations and be the prophetic person God is longing for you to be!
>
> Jesus was outdoors and surrounded by flowers as He gave the Sermon on the Mount and said: "Observe how the lilies of the field grow; they do not toil nor do they spin,

yet I say to you that not even Solomon in all his glory clothed himself like one of these (Matt. 6:28–29).

The great Master Artist calls our attention to the soulless flowers of the field, pointing out the beautiful tints and the wonderful variety of shades one flower may possess. Thus God has revealed His skill and care. Thus He would show the great love He has for every human being. The Lord our Creator expends as much care, wisdom and time upon the tiny flower as upon the great things He creates. In the tiniest flowers are seen a beauty and perfection that no human art can copy. The delicate tracery of the tinted rose, as well as the stars in the heavens, shows the penciling of the great Master Artist.

God desires us to bring fragrance into our life work. We are to be the planting of the Lord, serving Him in whatever way He wills. Let us do all in our power to beautify our character. Tender care must be given to the delicate plants. The bruised parts must be carefully bound up. So those who are weak in the faith must have fostering care. We are to bind to our stronger purposes those who are weak in the Lord's garden, giving them support. From the endless variety of plants and flowers, we may learn an important lesson. Blossoms are not the same in form or color. Some possess healing virtues. Some are always fragrant. Some open up for a short while—yet other flowers open up on a daily basis.

There are professing Christians who think it their duty to make every other Christian become like themselves. This is man's plan, not the plan of God. In the church of God there is room for characters as varied as are the flowers in a garden. In His spiritual garden there are many varieties of flowers.

SECURE IN YOUR IDENTITY

Whether male or female, we can be totally secure in our identity as chosen sons and daughters of the King. As the apostle Paul put it, "There is neither Jew nor Greek, there is neither slave nor free man, there is neither male nor female; for you are all one in Christ Jesus" (Gal. 3:28). We belong to Him, body, soul, and spirit, and we want Him to use us however He desires. One of *His* desires is that *we* would desire prophetic gifts that will enable us to teach and preach and interpret God's will and purpose for ourselves and others (see 1 Cor. 14:39).[2]

The Spirit invites us to be all that we can be in Christ Jesus. As men and women of faith, we are equals before Him, co-heirs of His grace and gifts. What a high calling!

LET'S PRAY

Father, we are thankful for all of the progress that has been made over the centuries and decades within the Church to ensure that women can be welcomed to become all they can be in Christ Jesus. We call forth prophetic women to be modern-day Annas, Deborahs, and Priscillas for the sake of this generation and the generations to come. Raise them up! May prophetic women everywhere flourish in a culture of honor to the end that they can influence every sphere of public and Church life, helping You to expand Your glorious Kingdom. For Jesus Christ's sake and in His name, Amen.

CHAPTER 9

INFLUENCING THE SEVEN SPHERES OF SOCIETY

*Then a shoot will spring from the stem of Jesse, and a branch
from his roots will bear fruit. The Spirit of the Lord will rest
on Him, the spirit of wisdom and understanding, the spirit
of counsel and strength, the spirit of knowledge and the fear
of the Lord. And He will delight in the fear of the Lord, and
He will not judge by what His eyes see, nor make a decision
by what His ears hear.*

ISAIAH 11:1–3

S even is not just a "lucky number"—it is considered to be the perfect number, the "number of fullness." The creation story is the first
appearance in the Bible of the number seven, when the time of rest
that God took on the seventh day gave form to the six-day workweek followed by a day of Sabbath rest. The seventh day was thereafter identified
with something being finished or completed, and God's people all over the
earth have had a seven-day week ever since.

Many of God's commands reflected the fullness of number seven: The Temple menorah had seven branches (see Exod. 25:37); animals had to be at least seven days old before they were sacrificed (see Exod. 22:30); and their blood was sprinkled seven times by the priests (see Lev. 4:17).

As we read through the Old Testament, we see that Joshua was commanded to march around the city of Jericho for seven days and on the seventh day to march around seven times, and that seven priests were to blow seven trumpets (see Josh. 6:3–4). Noah was instructed to shelter seven pairs of each clean animal on the ark (see Gen. 7:2). Proverbs 6:16 lists the "seven things the Lord hates."

In the New Testament, we find Jesus' seven miraculous signs in the Gospel of John,[1] seven parables in Matthew 13,[2] seven woes in Matthew 23,[3] and Jesus' seven last sayings on the cross (see all four Gospels).[4] Then we come to the book of Revelation, with sevens on almost every page—at least fifty times altogether (see, for example, Rev. 1:12, 16; 5:1; 8:2; 11:15; 15:7; 16:1; 21:9). Sometimes we find sevens clustered together in a single sentence: "The mystery of the seven stars that you saw in my right hand and of the seven golden lampstands is this: The seven stars are the angels of the seven churches, and the seven lampstands are the seven churches" (Rev. 1:20, NIV). We read about the Lamb in Heaven with His seven horns and seven eyes, sent out into the earth by the seven spirits of God:

> *I looked and saw a Lamb standing there before the twenty-four Elders, in front of the throne and the Living Beings, and on the Lamb were wounds that once had caused his death. He had seven horns and seven eyes, which represent the sevenfold Spirit of God, sent out into every part of the world. He stepped forward and took the scroll from the right hand of the one sitting upon the throne. And as he took the scroll, the twenty-four Elders fell down before the Lamb, each with a harp and golden vials filled with incense—the prayers of God's people!* (REV. 5:6–8, TLB)

The seven horns represent the fullness of power. The seven eyes indicate the fullness of insight. And fullness of worship is the only response. (Note that the vehicle for carrying the fullness of the radiating presence of Christ Jesus into the world is the prayers of God's people—yours and mine.)

In the Old Testament, multiples of seven keep occurring. For example, Jeremiah prophesied the duration of the Babylonian captivity of the people of Israel: seventy years, or seven times ten years (see Jer. 29:10). Daniel's prophecy about the seventy weeks is about seven times seven times ten, or four hundred and ninety years (see Dan. 9:24). The welcome Year of Jubilee (see Lev. 25:8) came after forty-nine years had been counted off (seven times seven). Whether used with literal meanings, as with the Year of Jubilee, or symbolic ones, as with Jesus' instruction to forgive "seventy times seven" (see Matt. 18:22), the resulting sense of well-rounded completion is unmistakable.

THE "SEVEN SPIRITS OF GOD"

Even with "seven" being used throughout the Bible, you almost never hear any preaching about the seven Spirits of God, despite prophetic Scriptures such as the one from Isaiah 11 above and others, such as the following:

> *To the leader of the church in Sardis write this letter: "This message is sent to you by the one who has the sevenfold Spirit of God and the seven stars..."* (REV. 3:1, TLB).

> *From the throne came flashes of lightning, rumblings and peals of thunder. In front of the throne, seven lamps were blazing. These are the seven spirits of God* (REV. 4:5, NIV).

Don't worry; these Scriptures are *not* referring to some little-known doctrine that increases the number of God's Holy Spirits from one to seven, making it the Trinity plus six. No, the "seven spirits of God" are seven aspects of His personality, seven fairly distinct expressions of the powerful nature of the Holy Spirit (and therefore seven "spirits" in a generalized sense of the word). We can glean the seven qualities directly from the Isaiah passage, where we can distinguish the following:

1. the Spirit of the Lord

2. the Spirit of wisdom

3. the Spirit of understanding

4. the Spirit of counsel

5. the Spirit of strength

6. the Spirit of knowledge

7. the Spirit of the Fear of the Lord

When you reread Isaiah 11:1–3 at the beginning of this chapter, at first you may think that Isaiah is listing only six expressions of the Spirit's nature. I used to wonder about that. Then I realized that the line that begins verse 2, "The Spirit of the Lord will rest on Him" actually represents one of the seven spirits of God. In other words, to my way of thinking, "the Spirit of the Lord" is the equivalent of the spirit of God's lordship. When you and I respond to this "lordship" aspect of the Holy Spirit, He in turn equips us to rule and reign in this life. It makes sense to me that the rest of the spirits of God—wisdom, understanding, strength, and the others—cannot be activated without that equipping spirit of lordship. Unless He is not only your Savior but your Lord and master, you are not going to be capable of following Him very well at all. In other words, He is either the Lord of all for you, or He is not your Lord at all.

The rest of the verse—while it applies most specifically to the coming Messiah, Jesus—applies to us as well, because the Messiah's Spirit dwells within us: "He will not judge by what His eyes see, nor make a decision by what His ears hear." In other words, our physical senses and capabilities are insufficient for making righteous judgments or wise decisions. We, like Jesus Himself, need the seven aspects of the Holy Spirit in order to function within the Kingdom of God. Our physical eyes must be informed by our spiritual eyes. Our physical ears must be enhanced and empowered by our spiritual ears. Our human strength is never enough to accomplish the work of God in the earth.

As prophetic people, we must always remember that just because something is "spiritual" does not mean that it comes from God. It is all too easy to get off the track, surrounded as we are by the insistent voices of the world, which is sold out to the devil. It is our job to prophesy true life to the broken, fragmented structures of human society.

The Lord is releasing the sights and sounds of Heaven all day long and throughout every night, and we need to pick them up. To be ready to receive what He has for us, our minds and spirits must be expanded into new dimensions. The Spirit of God is the only one who can do it, and once He does, our spirits will never shrink back to their original capacity. So do you want this? Are you ready for more?

SEVEN SPIRITS INTO SEVEN SPHERES OF SOCIETY

The idea of sevens extends into what many teachers have identified as the seven distinct spheres of society (also called the "seven cultural mountains" or, decades ago, they were referred to as the seven "mind molders.").[5] To each of these spheres of human civilization come all seven of the spirits of God. How? Through God's messengers, His faithful ones (you and me), and through His angels. We see it most clearly in the Revelation messages to the seven churches of Asia Minor, each of which had been assigned an angel (one of the seven stars): "The seven stars are the angels of the seven churches" (Rev. 1:20).

Today the Holy Spirit in all His fullness is being sent forth into the entire world as believers who are filled with His Spirit carry His impact and influence everywhere they go. Jesus dispatched His disciples to "go therefore and make disciples of all the nations" (Matt. 28:19) carrying the light of the world.

What are these seven spheres of society? They can be identified in brief by the following key words:

1. Family

2. Government

3. Education

4. Economy

5. Church/Religion

6. Arts and Entertainment

7. Media

To each of these seven spheres the prophetic people of God bring seven identifiable expressions of the prophetic spirit:

1. *Visionary leadership* (Because they can look into the future, these prophetic people can express the will of God and lead the way into the future.)

2. *Prophetic worship* (Prophetic worshipers help break open the land and help to bring others into the presence of God.)

3. *Prophetic intercession* (Prophetic intercessors pray God's promises back to Him so that He can fulfill His purposes in the earth.)

4. *Proclamation of God's corporate purpose* (Not limited to speaking personal prophecies only, these prophetic voices

speak to the whole Body of Christ or to secular society, proclaiming God's comprehensive purposes.)

5. *Proclamation of God's heart standards* (Ministries that teach about godly order and purity and also preachers of holiness proclaim the standards of God's heart to their sphere of influence.)

6. *Proclamation of the Church's social responsibilities* (More than the so-called "social gospel," which can seem incomplete to evangelical Christians, the evangelical and social justice emphases are combined here into a full gospel.)

7. *Proclamation of God's administrative strategies* (Prophetic administrators, men and women who have been gifted to create the "wineskins" for the Spirit-filled life, help enable the outworking of God's plan. Example: Joseph's Spirit-inspired solution averted starvation in the time of famine in Egypt.)

I have taught more about these seven expressions of the prophetic spirit under the category of "varieties of anointings" in books such as *The Seer.*

GREAT DIVERSITY OF PROPHETIC ANOINTING

I cannot emphasize enough how *big* God is. We see an almost bewildering variety of gifts, anointings, ministries, and combinations across the Body of Christ. Yet even with such diversity, everything is under the governance of the same Lord: "There are diversities of gifts, but the same Spirit. There are differences of ministries, but the same Lord. And there are diversities of activities, but it is the same God who works all in all" (1 Cor. 12:4–6, NKJV).

Before we go much further, we should ask, "What is an anointing, anyway?" My definition (which I developed as I worked on my books *Releasing*

Spiritual Gifts Today and *Living a Supernatural Life*) is as follows: "An anointing is the supernatural enablement, grace, and manifest presence of the Holy Spirit operating upon or through an individual or group to produce the works of Jesus."

Such a supernatural enablement or grace brings the presence of the Holy Spirit to bear upon countless situations. Energized by the same God and Father, prophetic believers bring forth a wide variety of gifts, ministries, and effects—always under the direction of the Spirit of the Lord God. (Read First Corinthians 12:4–6 again.) The way the Holy Spirit manifests Himself will look different in its expression from culture to culture, race to race, country to country, and from one denomination to another. That is to be expected—and celebrated! We have a great big God who can reach into all of the hidden places, public and private, with His love and power. Our part is to collaborate with Him, even across generational lines. Like the younger Aaron and Hur, holding up the hands of the older Moses (see Exod. 17:8–13),[6] we need to hold up the hands of those in authority for maximum impact.

We hold on to the Lord Jesus, who Himself was anointed by His Father God, as we operate under His anointing. With Him, we continue His works: "You know of Jesus of Nazareth, how God anointed Him with the Holy Spirit and with power, and how He went about doing good and healing all who were oppressed by the devil, for God was with Him" (Acts 10:38).

"The Anointing" is not some big, unattainable entity. It is something more like a Play-Doh factory—at least that is the way I have come to see it. Regardless of the kind of person you are and whatever tools God has hidden within you, He can mold and shape you for His divine purposes. You just have to make yourself available to Him and stay malleable. You see, as long as everything you do points back to Jesus and encourages others, you do not have to get tied up in trying to figure out which category you fall into. In all likelihood, it will keep changing anyway. "The prophetic" is just not as narrow a track as I used to think it was. (We're finally moving away from the idea that the prophetic is about "platform." Rather, it is about stewardship of what God has given each one of us. I wish I had known that forty or fifty years ago when I first embarked on this adventure with Him.)

Some of us have been placed in the Church to minister mostly to the rest of the Body of Christ. Others have been anointed as "sent ones" to reach into the secular community outside the Church.

In the past few years, I have been prophesying and teaching about "Kingdom consultants" or "prophetic solutionists"—prophetic men and women whose ministry is not confined to the "church mountain" but rather extends into a wide variety of secular settings. Their expertise and sensitivity to the Spirit enable them to advise and influence and effect change (sometimes at high levels) in government, economy, education, media, and more.

These anointed men and women of God are part of the Church but not stuck there. In the past I referred to Kingdom consultants as "hope ambassadors." God gives them moments of prophetic revelation that can be turned into movements of prophetic reformation. They are Kingdom administrators, shedding the powerful light of God into dark places that up to that time have been devoid of Kingdom influence. They possess keen insight and they develop inspired strategies that make true Kingdom-oriented reformation possible in places that may never have uttered the name of Jesus.

They are walking in the footsteps of the "great ones" such as Joseph, Daniel, Esther, Ezra, and Nehemiah. They find themselves in situations not of their own choosing but they recognize that they have been positioned by God "for such a time as this" (Esther 4:14). Like Queen Esther, they take it upon themselves to surrender to God's guidance and come up with radical solutions, sometimes sticking their necks out and taking big risks. An example would be William Wilberforce, the English MP whose lifelong commitment and prodigious efforts led to many moral reforms, most importantly the abolishment of slavery in England in 1834.

Kingdom consultants do not have to be queens or priests or rulers themselves. In a way, God calls all of us to be Kingdom consultants, if we take the Great Commission seriously (see Matt. 28:18–20). As we proceed through our lives, relating to people in our wide variety of secular work-places, each one of us is called to spread Kingdom influence. The *only* way we can do it is with the King's assistance. We are conduits of His love and power. Over time, God can use us to bring urgently needed changes to the world outside the Church.

As vessels of the prophetic anointing, only a few of us at any given time carry out a governmental leadership role akin to that of Moses, Abraham, and David. Most of us do not and should not try to exercise leadership but rather only to release the revelation God gives us to allow God's presence to make an impact wherever things would otherwise remain isolated from Him. We cannot and should not covet each other's grace allotment.

As a prophetic individual, just make yourself available to God and stay flexible. You never know when you might meet an influential person or find yourself behind the scenes where you can pray and exercise Kingdom influence!

HOW ARE YOU WIRED PROPHETICALLY?

I remember walking into a conference in Minneapolis. I saw this lady up on the platform and she was painting a picture. I could tell immediately that she had received professional training, and that she had surrendered her gifts to a specialized prophetic anointing. She was "painting in the Spirit" with skill and grace. Many prophetic people are artists, poets, singers, musicians, and artisans. The Lord takes their sensitivity and training and couples it with His anointing to bring them into places where they can have real influence on the society around them for the sake of His Kingdom.

I have tried to encourage my own children in this regard. All of them are gifted artistically and as the adult children of a man who is identified as a prophet they understood that they should not do exactly what I do. From film editing to art therapy to 3D animation to songwriting, the four of them give expression to the heart of God and influence the spheres of entertainment, the arts, media, the Church, and family.

I live in the Nashville, Tennessee area, Music City, U.S.A. So many of the people in this city are actually called prophetically by God, but they do not understand that realm and they often mess up because they are so sensitive. They are wired in a certain way and they may never have found a safe place within the Body of Christ to be prophetic musicians. Even if you do not consider yourself a prophetic artist, you can make room for others simply by being aware of this expression of God's Spirit. I so appreciate the diversity within the Body!

Besides prophetic artists, I can identify several other prophetic categories that blend gifting and training with prophetic instincts. We have prophetic writers who express prophetic messages best in written form; in fact they are often better at writing something than they are at speaking in public. When they write, whether they pen books, articles, poems, or song lyrics, they express the heart of God to contemporary society.

We also have prophetic teachers. They are not merely prophets who happen to be asked to teach something, but teachers whose subject matter comes alive under God's anointing. The content of their teaching shines with clarity and applicability. Truly they are a valuable gift to the Body of Christ.

The anointing of a prophetic teacher may or may not overlap somewhat with that of a prophetic evangelist or a prophetic counselor. What is a prophetic evangelist? Prophetic evangelists are the ones who step out into places where they can interact with the people who have not yet responded to the Gospel message. They are not afraid of the unknown as they work (most effectively teamed up with others) to speak prophetically on the streets, retail stores, health clubs, and neighborhoods of their God-assigned localities. Often enough, signs and wonders occur as they share the love of Christ, and they can carry the Good News right into newly opened hearts.

Prophetic counselors rarely work in such a public way unless they are also teachers. Usually working one on one, prophetic counselors understand what an integrated model of wholeness looks like. They are able to combine their spiritual gifts with professional training to help bring people's hearts and minds into alignment with the love and will of God.

I believe that there are even prophetic entrepreneurs! I do not mean to imply that all entrepreneurs out there are anointed by God to initiate new ideas. But an increasing number of them are inventive people who live on the curve of discovery. Energized by the Spirit, they start new businesses, patent new inventions, and bring forth prophetic solutions to today's practical needs. They do something to benefit others with their inspired ideas.

Then there are those special people whom I call prophetic Spirit-bearers. They not only practice the presence of God in their own lives, but they also release supernatural manifestations of God's glorious presence wherever they walk. Sometimes drastic responses occur: falling in the Spirit, quaking and shaking, ecstatic speech, and more. When they show up, so do power encounters, angelic activity, and kingdom clashes. Prophetic Spirit-bearers go with the wind of the Spirit (see John 3:8). In the experience of my lifetime, one of the most effective prophetic Spirit-bearers was the late Jill Austin. She must have had special angels assigned to her, because God's fire fell wherever she ministered. She was a prophetic Spirit-bearer.

What I am trying to show is how, when a prophetic anointing saturates a blend of spiritual and natural gifts, you will see God in action—guaranteed. It makes you wonder: What kind of prophet am I and where have I been assigned? The enemy may try to keep you from grasping your call or stop you from fulfilling it, but if you cling closely to God, He will see you through.

SEEK HIM

Our heavenly Father always gives good gifts to His children and to those who ask (see Matt. 7:10 and Luke 11:11).[7] Sometimes the only reason we cannot see our gifts in a prophetic light is because we have not asked to see them with God's eyes. In other words, we have not because we ask not (see James 4:2).

Let's not limit the empowering work of the seven Spirits of God to what we have been exposed to in the past, whether our experiences have been positive or negative. Let's plunge in. Let's go deeper. Do not get tied up in knots about which gift or what kind of a call you may have. God is going to express Himself through whatever He has made you to be, so you can find peace in that knowledge and be at complete liberty to respond to Him.

Stretch out your heart and say, "Lord, I ask You to express Your prophetic Spirit through me." He wants to do that in as many diverse ways as there are people, as there are personalities, as there are gift mixes across the face of the earth. Allow your hunger and thirst to rise up. May your prayers rise like incense into Heaven, all the way into the very heart of God, so that He can anoint you and equip you for much more. You were created for something special in the Kingdom. Lean into Him until you find out what it is and then keep leaning on Him for the strength and wisdom you will need to walk it out.

LET'S PRAY

Father, in Jesus' mighty name, we welcome the seven Spirits of God into our lives. We want to see the revelatory gifts of Your Holy Spirit operating in our lives so that, through us, You can make an impact on the culture and human life around us. We want to combine our efforts with those of like-minded and like-hearted others so that together we can affect every sphere of the society we live in: family, government, education, economy, Church, arts, and media. We pray that You will release us along with other prophetic artists, prophetic writers, prophetic teachers, prophetic evangelists, prophetic counselors, prophetic entrepreneurs, and prophetic Spirit-bearers, all of us equipped with the sevenfold Spirit of God. For Jesus Christ's sake, Amen.

PART FOUR

PROPHETIC
COMMISSIONING

CHAPTER 10

FROM SURRENDER TO SENT ONES

The Lord was with Samuel as he grew up, and he let none of Samuel's words fall to the ground. And all Israel from Dan to Beersheba recognized that Samuel was attested as a prophet of the Lord. The Lord continued to appear at Shiloh, and there he revealed himself to Samuel through his word.

1 SAMUEL 3:19–21, NIV

I want to tell you a true story about my friend Ché Ahn, who is a modern-day apostle and founder of Harvest International Ministries.[1] Once I was with him in Huntsville, Alabama in a church that was not very big. (Both of us like to accept invitations to minister to smaller gatherings sometimes, not only to large ones.) There was a dinner before a small group meeting. At the end of the meal, some of the church leaders had to leave the room for a time, and Ché very naturally rose from the table and began to clear and clean the tables. That is just the way he is. If somebody had said to him, "Wait, you're an apostle. You should not have to do this kind of service," he would have said something like, "Well, so...?" Ché was not concerned with hierarchical positions; he was expressing his heart as a servant. He is a very busy man with many responsibilities, but he does not consider cleaning tables to be beneath him.

Sometimes we need to be reminded of this. We forget that God's Kingdom incorporates countless opportunities to serve. Before Philip was ever an evangelist, he was first a deacon, a servant to the church body. He used the gifts God had given him to serve his brothers and sisters in the local church. I do not think he expected to become an itinerant evangelist, but when it was time, he was ready. He took his servant's heart with him. He is a good example of someone who recognized that his commissioning as a deacon did not relegate him to the same role forever. Once a deacon, always a deacon? No. But once a servant, yes, always a servant.

We need to recognize the progressive steps that we take as we nurture a prophetic call. In the prophetic calling, as with any office or ministry gift, first you are called and then trained. Eventually, you are commissioned. These are not just one-time steps (which is often the way we think about them). They may be repeated several times in the life of an individual. That makes them progressive. Far from being static, the gifts and callings of God are dynamic and full of life.

Yet in order to be obedient to God and an influencer in our sphere, we sometimes need to talk to ourselves—even prophesy over ourselves—about the message of this chapter. We need to lay hands on ourselves and say, "Now out of my innermost being is coming forth rivers of living water." I am not advocating becoming a Lone Ranger, separate from your local Body of Christ—not at all. I'm just saying that sometimes we need to wake ourselves up in the Lord. We need to give ourselves to Him once again so He can lead us up higher.

We read that "David strengthened himself in the Lord his God" (1 Sam. 30:6). We need to do likewise. And, like the disciples who became apostles, along with Jesus Himself, we need to remember that "The greatest among you must be a servant" (Matt. 23:11, NLT).

Some people get too big, too important, in their own eyes. I know that you and I are called to greatness in the Kingdom of God, but that is not the same as being famous or lording it over others self-importantly. We remain servants always, even as we grow in response to the Spirit's actions in our lives. We keep a serving towel over our arm; it becomes part of our attire. We are never too high to take the trash out, or whatever. In reality, part of our authority will come from our humility.

As my late wife, Michal Ann, used to say: "God is not looking for people with big gifts or special callings. He is looking for people with big hearts who will love the one who is in front them." Then she would add, "Just do it."

THE PROPHETIC CALLING

As you think about scriptural examples and experiences from everyday life, you find many different ways that people have been called into prophetic ministry. Some seem to be born with a gift, while others are "born again with a gift" or "baptized in the Spirit with a gift." Still other callings and gifts emerge gradually over time, even late in life. Each one of us was divinely called before we were born, but our personal development proceeds at varying rates. Some of us recognize God's call in childhood, others not until mature adulthood.

The prophet Jeremiah's call came before he was conceived (see Jer. 1:5). So did John the Baptist's call: "when Elizabeth heard the greeting of Mary... the babe leaped in her womb" (Luke 1:41, NKJV). The prophet Samuel's call came when he was quite young (see 1 Sam. 3:1–20). The prophet Elisha's call came when he was a full-grown man, while he was plowing a field (see 1 Kings 19:19–21). Amos never prophesied until he had worked for a time as a herdsman and a grower of figs (see Amos 1:1; 7:12–15).

How will you know when your call comes? I can think of at least seven ways:

1. Supernatural events occur, including visitations of angels or Jesus Himself (see Isa. 6:1; Jer. 1:4; 1 Sam. 3:1–4; Acts 9:3–6).

2. People will begin to tell you (see 1 Sam. 3:20).

3. Leaders will recognize it (see Prov. 18:16).

4. You may receive an initial prophecy about the future. (Review the life stories of Isaiah, Jeremiah, Samuel, and Zechariah.)

5. Through others' spiritual gifts, you may be called into something new (see Acts 13:1–3; 2 Tim. 1:6).

6. God will confirm a call through more than one witness and through His written Word (see 2 Cor. 13:1).

7. Fruit will begin to be borne (see Mark 16:20).

I believe that often when you are called to an influential public prophetic ministry, God often starts early in your life, even miraculously. One dramatic example is Paul Cain, who has prophesied with a level of accuracy that most of us will never achieve. When his mother, Anna, was carrying him more than eighty years ago, she had several terminal illnesses, cancer being one of them. She was on her deathbed. An angel came into the bedroom and told her that she would live and not die, and that her unborn baby would be a son who would preach the Gospel like Paul. She was divinely healed of her terminal diseases and she did give birth to a son—whom she named Paul—and he became a forerunner for the modern-day seer-prophets. (His mother went on to see her hundredth birthday!)

The late Bob Jones grew up in Arkansas, in the country. As a seven-year-old kid, he was walking on a dirt road one day when the archangel Gabriel showed up on a white horse and blew a trumpet. It scared the daylights out of little Bob and he ran in terror. He was so scared that he never surrendered to the call of God until later in his life, but when he did, his prophetic gift was truly remarkable, as many people can verify.

Another prominent modern-day prophetic voice was John Paul Jackson, whom we call an "eleventh-hour prophet" because he was always speaking out prophetically about current events and the end times. His longsuffering mother carried him two months longer than is normal for pregnancy—for eleven long months! Her due date was May 30, 1950, and she went into labor that day. But then inexplicably her labor pains ceased, and John Paul was not born until July 30 (at 11:55 P.M.)—two months late, to the very day, an eleven-month pregnancy.[2] Before she got pregnant, she had been given a prophetic word to the effect that her son was going to be an eleventh-hour prophetic voice.

In Chapter 4 I told about how my favorite teacher and my great-grandmother predicted my future calling. But before I was born, something else foreshadowed it, although I will never claim the higher status of the prophets I just told you about. My parents had two daughters and my mother had been praying for a son. She got pregnant again, but miscarried a baby boy. She felt she had lost her prayed-for son, but she prayed again for another son, saying, "Lord, if you will give me another son, I will dedicate him to Christ's service." Exactly a year to the day of her miscarriage, I was born. Since my mother's name is Amanda Elizabeth, which means "grace" and "consecrated one," I always say that by grace I came forth into consecration.

Growing up, I talked to God all the time. I considered Him my best friend; I felt I was called to be a friend of God. Then when I got filled with the Holy Spirit in 1972, I just bubbled over and I began to prophesy, without even really knowing what "prophecy" was. Now I have spent my entire life in Christ's service as my mother prayed I would, and I am not finished serving Him yet!

TRAINING AND MATURING
IN THE PROPHETIC CALL

Once we have become aware that God has given us a prophetic gift, we need to learn how to use it. Books like this one can make up part of the learning process, but we need to seek out specific training so that we can mature in our prophetic call.

Over recent decades we have seen a welcome increase in teaching and mentoring for some of the other spiritual gifts such as the gift of pastor (and even for apostolic builders) along with the gifts of evangelism and teacher. But up until recently, there has been relatively poor "father-modeling" for people to help them nurture a prophetic call. Thus you and I must pay extra attention to learning about what our prophetic call entails.

We might assume that our maturity in the prophetic call is tied to our experience over many years and that it corresponds more or less to our physical and mental and emotional maturity. But this is not always the case. Prophetic gifts are just that—gifts, sovereignly bestowed. They are not given only to those who deserve them or even to those who will steward them well. They are freely given by the Father as He wills. I know a woman who stepped into full-blown prophetic giftedness at a level of consistent accuracy and detail that I have never achieved in my whole lifetime. It almost made me jealous, considering how long and hard my road has been. But it is God's prerogative to do it that way. Gifts are *gifts*, not rewards.

Wherever we serve, we must do all we can to foster a love-based prophetic culture. "Let all that you do be done with love" (1 Cor. 16:14, NKJV), including all that you do prophetically.

Always watch out for self-righteousness. It is such a major hindrance to the development of the prophetic gift, not to mention to character development. The gift that was freely given to you is not to be worn as a badge that proves your merit and praiseworthiness. God loves you as a prophet because He made you that way, but He gave you the gift for the sake of the people around you, not for your personal self-esteem.

All of us need to grow and mature in our use of prophetic gifts, and our growth needs to be intentional. Maturity of character and wisdom are not automatically conferred on recipients of the gift. Many, although not all, prophetic people start out with a natural sensitivity of spirit that can enhance their prophetic receptivity. Other personality traits may or may not seem to go with the prophetic gift. In every case, wherever we are weak, God will supply strength. Remember that God selected Saul (Paul), a hard-line Jewish scholar, to bring the Gospel to the Gentiles. Paul had no natural affinity for Gentiles, but he surrendered himself to God and God equipped him to penetrate the hard hearts of unreached people in places that were far from Jerusalem and away from the Roman province of Judea.

The key is our surrender. As it is often stated, "Gifts are given. Fruits are grown." Called and sent out to bear fruit for the Kingdom, we must learn how to do it as we go. "Go and grow" could be our motto.

We must press forward with intentionality. Paul urged his young friend Timothy to "kindle afresh the gift of God" that God had given him when Paul prayed for him with the laying on of hands (see 2 Tim. 1:6). He also reminded Timothy not to neglect the spiritual gift God had bestowed upon him when the elders of the Church had laid hands on him in prayer (see 1 Tim. 4:14).

We need to remind ourselves that God moves sovereignly to bestow gifts, graces, ministries, and offices entirely as He desires, giving little or no consideration to the condition of the person. We see this throughout Church history and throughout Scripture. (See, for example, Acts 2:1–4; 4:32; 10:44.) Sometimes the bestowal of gifts comes through the laying on of hands in prayer, which is what happened for Timothy. We see this throughout the history of the people of God. God transmitted gifts to Joshua through Moses' hands (see Deut. 34:9). He used the church at Antioch to commission Barnabas and Paul (see Acts 13:1–3) and the

Jerusalem church to set apart Stephen, Phillip, and the other early deacons (see Acts 6:3–6). Paul was struck down by the power of God on the road to Damascus, but he could get back on his feet and be sent out only after the faithful disciple Ananias laid hands on him (see Acts 9:17). The laying on of hands should not be done indiscriminately or hastily (see 1 Tim. 5:22), but it remains an important component of the process of activating a spiritual gift.

Thankfully, mentoring is often a large part of the learning process. We can look to Jesus and His disciples for the best example. First, Jesus called them to follow Him, and the men exemplified quite a range of natural qualities. Because several of them were fishermen by trade, He told them, "Follow Me, and I will make you fishers of men" (Matt. 4:19). That word "make" is significant. It implies training. He did not say, "Follow Me as disciples and I will *gift* you...." He passed on His authority to His disciples, and He gave them instructions. He expected them to begin to learn from experience. Note that He did not limit this call to His primary twelve disciples. Here is the account:

> *The Lord now chose seventy other disciples and sent them on ahead in pairs to all the towns and villages he planned to visit later. These were his instructions to them: "Plead with the Lord of the harvest to send out more laborers to help you, for the harvest is so plentiful and the workers so few. Go now, and remember that I am sending you out as lambs among wolves. Don't take any money with you, or a beggar's bag, or even an extra pair of shoes. And don't waste time along the way. Whenever you enter a home, give it your blessing. If it is worthy of the blessing, the blessing will stand; if not, the blessing will return to you. When you enter a village, don't shift around from home to home, but stay in one place, eating and drinking without question whatever is set before you. And don't hesitate to accept hospitality, for the workman is*

worthy of his wages! If a town welcomes you, follow these two rules:

(1) Eat whatever is set before you.

(2) Heal the sick; and as you heal them, say, 'The Kingdom of God is very near you now.'

"But if a town refuses you, go out into its streets and say, 'We wipe the dust of your town from our feet as a public announcement of your doom. Never forget how close you were to the Kingdom of God!'" (LUKE 10:1–11, TLB)

After they went out boldly and ministered, they returned to report their successes (see Luke 10:17).[3] This proves that Jesus' training process was effective.

In a similar way, the prophet Elijah raised up Elisha to be his successor. First he anointed him (see 1 Kings 19:15–16), and then he cast his mantle upon him (see 1 Kings 19:19). For a considerable time, Elisha became Elijah's servant (see 1 Kings 19:21). Then, after years of training—by example and demonstration, all "show and tell," not book-learning—and certain tests of endurance and persistence, Elisha was able to obtain Elijah's mantle for good when he watched him ascend into Heaven. Then he proceeded to embark upon his own ministry (see 2 Kings 2:1–12).

Ask the Father to send you a mentor—or more than one of them. Do not limit Him; He may decide to answer that prayer in a unique way. But He will answer it. Just as He brings forth a wide variety of gift-blends, so he also trains us in a diversity of ways. He does not want you to become a carbon copy of anybody else, although He does want you to imitate the *faith* of those who have paved the way before you (see Heb. 13:7).[4] Just because your prophetic mentor uses certain words and phrases does not mean that you need to use the same ones. Just because he or she dresses a certain way does not mean you need to change your wardrobe. The important thing is faith. Imitate your mentor's life of prayer. Find out how to add fasting to your praying. Find out how your mentor relates to his or her spouse. Celebrate the spontaneous, creative aspects of the person's gifting and be ready for God to launch you in your own identity as a prophetic individual.

As we grow in our own gifts and graces from our Father, we need to be able to see good examples of how others have matured. They provide a kind of scaffolding or framework for our lives while the cement is being poured into the foundation of our lives. That framework can be removed once the cement has tempered and firmed up, and we can proceed to build on top of it.

You do learn methodologies and techniques from your mentors. But the primary thing you learn is how to stay in hot pursuit of your relationship with God. He is your source!

GROWING IN MATURITY

It takes time to grow in maturity. With purposeful attention, the gifts that come from God can develop into maturity. With practice, prophetic people can become more sensitive to the voice of God and more accurate in hearing Him. This occurs as the strength of our faith increases and through our active obedience in "doing what the Father is doing" (see John 5:19) and through our attention to regular prayer and fasting and other forms of self-restraint. Character growth arises from the soil of accurate doctrine and familiarity with the written Word of God.

We have a saying: "Practice makes perfect." That is true in a way, but my version of that saying is: "Practice brings us to a higher realm." Actually, perfection is not my goal. My goal is a higher realm. I never want to be a perfectionist. I will not wait for the next big heavenly "download," either, because I know I would be disappointed when it does not happen. I need to take what I have been given and do with it what I believe God wants me to do. I need to be faithful with my "little" so that He may make me rule over much (see Matt. 25:21, 23). Jesus taught the principle that faithfulness brings increase, and that can be applied to our growth in the use of our prophetic gift.

Growth in maturity involves the development of strong character, and this character is absolutely vital for prophets. God does not want us only to give messages to people; He wants us to become a living word to the people around us. Any truly prophetic person will learn to love the cross of Christ and will come to appreciate even the most excruciating lessons in character development. I have seen my friend Patricia King actually kiss the cross over and over and over. That says something about her character and it makes me able to trust the words from God that she brings.

Character is seldom revealed until tests and trials come. At such times spiritual gifts may seem to "dry up" and disappear as God's pruning process does its work. But once the season of pruning has been completed, the gifts will flow again, with greater purity, accuracy, and impact. The vessel that carries the living water of Christ will be cleaner than it was before.

None of us can grow apart from others. We are each a small part of a living Body, and we need each other. Each of us needs to be accountable to others in all of the areas of our natural and spiritual life: our motives and our behavior, our finances, our morality. Is this too much to expect? Paul did not think so. He wrote: "We, being many, are one body in Christ, and individually members of one another" (Rom. 12:5, NKJV). And "all of you together are Christ's body, and each of you is a part of it" (1 Cor. 12:27, NLT).

Paul did not tire of repeating himself: "And concerning you, my brethren, I myself also am convinced that you yourselves are full of goodness, filled with all knowledge and able also to admonish one another" (Rom. 15:14). He went on to write, "Therefore encourage one another and build up one another, just as you also are doing" (1 Thess. 5:11). The writer of the letter to the Hebrews added, "You must warn each other every day, while it is still 'today,' so that none of you will be deceived by sin and hardened against God" (Heb. 3:13, NLT). This is only a selection from the many Scriptures about the interdependence of the members of the Body of Christ. Nobody ever grows and matures in isolation.

When you combine your efforts with others' you learn how to give honor to them instead of being in competition with them or jealous of them. As you grow in righteousness, you stop coveting the giftings, status, roles, positions, titles, functions, or prestige of others. You learn to value humility as God's love goes deep inside you. Through experience, you learn to wait patiently for God's timing, which always proves to be so much better than your own.

When I think about waiting for God's timing, I always think of the prophet Jeremiah. Just look at the progression of his prophetic life, and the patient humility he had to learn. The Lord first spoke to Jeremiah in about 627 B.C., the "thirteenth year of Josiah" (see Jer. 25:3). But it was not until fifteen years later, in 612 B.C., that he began to prophesy in public. Then the next year, when certain tablets of the Law were found, the king did not consult the prophet Jeremiah but rather Huldah, a woman who was a prophetess (see 2 Kings 22). Apparently at that point his reputation was less than hers and the king thought she might be a bit more sympathetic. Still, Jeremiah went on to prophesy to small and great for many more years, and he was faithful even in the face of repudiation and even maltreatment. Early on, he resigned himself to be faithful to the difficult role to which God had assigned him, as we see here:

> *Jeremiah the prophet spoke to all the people of Judah and to all the inhabitants of Jerusalem, saying, "From the thirteenth year of Josiah the son of Amon, king of Judah, even to this day, these twenty-three years the word of the Lord has come to me, and I have spoken to you again and again, but you have not listened. And the Lord has sent to you all His servants the prophets again and again, but you have not listened nor inclined your ear to hear* (JER. 25:2–4).

Each of us will have many challenges to face as we learn to follow the Lord obediently, and He will use every one to mature us so that we can bear fruit for His Kingdom.

For sure it is harder to gauge the progress and growth of one's character compared to other kinds of growth, because character traits are invisible for the most part. Motives are the hardest to recognize. A true prophetic word can be given out of an impure motive of self-promotion, which may be detected by the hearers and not by the prophet. This makes it all-important to keep surrendering everything to the Lord, including our unmet needs, unhealed wounds, and unhealthy upbringing. We do not have to understand ourselves in order to surrender ourselves to His shepherding and fatherly care.

WISDOM OF THE WORD

Surrendering ourselves to God includes surrendering ourselves to His living Word. (The Word is both Jesus Himself, as we read in John 1:1, and the sixty-six books of the Bible.) The Scriptures provide us with a living road map that keeps us on track as the Spirit highlights one part after another. The wisdom of the Word is as rich and inexhaustible as it is reliable!

To be consistently effective as workers in God's harvest, I am convinced that we must become totally *addicted* to the Word of God. It must become our food and drink, our sustenance. Too many revelatory-gifted people use the Scriptures primarily as their source of validation for their latest "revelation." They tend to stretch the Scriptures improperly to fit their latest dream or vision, and they do not "study to show themselves approved" (see 2 Tim. 2:15).

To avoid this temptation, we must always maintain a devotional life that continues regardless of the ebbs and flows of our ministry life. Never mistake ministry for devotion. Read and meditate on the Scriptures for your own life. Feed yourself first, before you try to feed others spiritually.

Learn to love being with Him, and become more impressed with the word He stirs up in your heart than with the words coming out through your mouth.

Always stick with the "main and plain" principles of Scripture. Root yourself in sound doctrine in the basics of the faith, things such as Jesus' virgin birth, His cross, His resurrection from the dead, His second coming, being "born again," the inspiration of the Scriptures, and so on. Do not accept every new twist to the age-old, foundational beliefs of the historic Church. Instead, seek out an appropriate historical and contextual understanding of the Scriptures, and let the Holy Spirit bring you into a current-day application. Unless you are grounded in proper biblical doctrine, your interpretation of revelation might become tainted. Over time, you could wander far from the straight and narrow way of Jesus.

Furthermore, it is important for revelatory-gifted people who have a public voice to ally themselves if possible with teachers who are more systematically trained in understanding Scripture and theology. This is for balance, protection, and enhancement of God's message.

Always use the written Word to judge and assess the spoken word, and do it responsibly, taking to heart the fact that you are stewarding a gift from God and therefore ultimately responsible to Him.

It is prudent to accumulate resources that can help you understand the symbols and types of the Old Testament as used in the New Testament. The Word is an integral part of the Kingdom of God, and you may not come to the right conclusions about contemporary revelatory experiences unless you understand hidden biblical meanings. Such knowledge is a valuable tool for your prophetic toolkit.[5]

In summary, I cannot overstress the importance of maintaining both mental and spiritual preparedness through the regular exercise of spiritual disciplines. That is the better part of seeking God's presence and surrendering yourself to Him on a daily basis. When the fullness of timing meets the fullness of preparation in the wisdom ways of God, the atmosphere is ripe for the "suddenlies" of God, when all things are possible!

ADMINISTERING THE PROPHETIC GIFT

There is so much to learn. Together with like-minded others, we must seek the Lord to forge ahead in our lives in the Spirit and the Word, asking Him to enable us to reflect His character and love through our words and actions.

Maturing in wisdom includes maturing in our presentation of God's word. Most of the time, the presentation of the revelation is as important as the revelation itself. There is so much to learn and to keep in mind. Here is a summary for your reference:

1. The prophetic person must learn to overcome fears and failures of the past so that they affect him less and less as he or she matures. This includes fear from past hurts, past deceptions, past corruptions and sins, and the past control of other people.

2. The prophetic person must learn to overcome his or her distinct set of hindrances to delivering trustworthy revelations. The most common hindrances fall into three categories: (a) spirit or soul wounds, (b) preconceived opinions, and (c) legalism and argumentativeness.

3. The prophetic person must learn the value of holding his or her tongue. The practice of self-restraint exemplifies the fruit of the Spirit called patience and self-control. A good part of this restraint involves honoring authority at all times and in all places.

4. The prophetic person must never use revelation as a tool of gossip or for undermining someone destructively. The whole purpose of a gift of the Spirit is to edify, exhort, and comfort, always in love (see 1 Cor. 14:3).

5. The prophetic person does not need to utter everything he or she knows. (A fool opens his mouth and tells all he knows, as Proverbs 29:11 says.) Learning restraint is part of learning how to keep a word until its proper time, avoiding premature release and confusion. It always means avoiding being cocky, coy, prideful, or arrogant.

6. The prophetic person learns to recognize the difference between revelation and authority, why one prophet is "heard" while another is not. The authority to be heard comes from a relational joining with God Himself along with His confirmation of a revelation through His written Word and through others. There is no room for competition or jealousy. The fruit of a delivered word must always increase faith and encourage the hearers.

7. The prophetic person learns the limits of the sphere of authority given by God. The sphere may be as small as a family or as large as international affairs, ranging from local small groups, congregations, or cities to translocal states, regions, or nations.

BEING A SENT ONE

In your life and ministry as a prophetic person, you may see progressive releases and times of commissioning. Being "sent" never happens once for all time because the Kingdom of God is dynamic and relational. You are called the first time, and you continue to be called. You are trained in some things, and you continue to be trained. You are sent out and then you are brought back again to be re-trained, re-tooled, and re-envisioned so that you can be re-commissioned with fresh purpose and power.

Only God can commission you, and only God can back up His words. When He backs them up, they do not fail. Then other people will recognize the power, accuracy, and consistency of the words you deliver and they will pay attention to what you say and do. If you have been truly commissioned by God, He will speak to you through various means, consistently.

You will not be sent out into the wilderness on your own. Resist the prophetic tendency to alienate yourself from others. Go forth with the assurance that God is with you. Rejoice! Just "do the stuff," as John Wimber used to say. Be sure to ask for intercessory covering when you undertake special ventures. Recognize that each venture is different and that you will have to wear different "hats" or "shoes" for different events, time periods, and places. Be flexible—but always stay within your sphere of operation and strength.

Lastly, remember that you are a natural person. Value ordinary life and take time for play and work and all aspects of everyday living. Yes, you must embrace the purpose of pain in the process of maturing as a prophetic person. But you must always become better, not bitter.

Kiss the cross—and get splinters in your mouth! When you do, you will become a much better mouthpiece for God.

LET'S PRAY

Father, in the wonderful name of the Lord Jesus Christ, we choose to embrace our prophetic callings along with the numerous stages of training necessary for becoming an authentic "sent one." Holy Spirit, we ask You to move across the Body of Christ globally and to raise up many Shilohs, many safe places of equipping where the Samuels who have been called out of this generation can be confirmed, strengthened, established, and sent out. We surrender our all to Your call, trusting that You will help us grow and become all that You desire us to be. Thank You for the mighty work of grace in each of our lives. Again we say, Amen!

CHAPTER 11

LEARNING WAYS
OF WISDOM

*And Jesus increased in wisdom and stature, and in favor with
God and men.*

LUKE 2:52, NKJV

The spirit of wisdom is one of the seven Spirits of God that I intro-
duced to you in Chapter 9 because wisdom is one of the primary
qualities of God's Holy Spirit. He is wisdom personified, and "God
has united you with Christ Jesus. For our benefit God made him to be wisdom itself" (1 Cor. 1:30, NLT). I would say that wisdom is even more vital
to prophetic people than the divine revelation they receive, because only
through God-sent wisdom can they know how to handle the word of the
Lord in just the right way.

Okay, but how can we best lay hold of God's wisdom? We already know
we need to surrender ourselves to His lordship and to lean on Him continually, but does that guarantee that His wisdom will flow into our lives? What
should we expect? How can we recognize God's wisdom once it comes?

How does this wisdom come to us? Is it a sovereign gift from God? Is it a spiritual presence of some sort? Is our personal wisdom assembled from much reading and studying? Or does it come mostly from experience, from spending years in the School of Hard Knocks?

There is no one answer, because wisdom comes through all the above. We can see that when we simply search for the word "wisdom" in Scripture. Consider the following:

Wisdom as a gift:

For to one is given the word of wisdom through the Spirit, and to another the word of knowledge according to the same Spirit (1 COR. 12:8).

Wisdom as a spirit:

The Spirit of the Lord will rest on Him, the spirit of wisdom and understanding, the spirit of counsel and strength, the spirit of knowledge and the fear of the Lord (ISA. 11:2).

Wisdom from studying:

Study to shew thyself approved unto God, a workman that needeth not to be ashamed, rightly dividing the word of truth (2 TIM. 2:15, KJV).

Wisdom arising from life experience:

For a righteous man falls seven times, and rises again, but the wicked stumble in time of calamity (PROV. 24:16).

Even fools are thought wise when they keep silent; with their mouths shut, they seem intelligent (PROV. 17:28, NLT).

If our dear Lord Jesus, as we see in the short passage of Scripture at the beginning of this chapter, "increased" and grew in wisdom, stature, and favor with God and men, then we should expect to do so, as well. I think that is remarkable—that Jesus, who was God in the flesh, *kept increasing* in His wisdom throughout His life on earth.

Our increase in wisdom will not happen automatically, though. Like me, you surely have met people you knew many years before, perhaps when you were in high school, and you have been dismayed to see that they never matured much at all. They still act like teenagers who are "wet behind the ears," even though they may have a diploma, a career, a family, and a nice car. They do not even realize that they lack the mature wisdom that their years could have won for them.

I know that Scripture says "the fear of the Lord is the beginning of wisdom" (Prov. 9:10), so humble surrender to God must be the first step. I also know we need all the wisdom we can get and that we never have enough of it as long as we are alive on this earth. The apostle James clearly stated that we must *ask* for more wisdom—and that if you do, God will grant it to you: "If any of you lacks wisdom, let him ask of God, who gives to all generously and without reproach, and it will be given to him" (James 1:5). Even King Solomon, who was famous for his unsurpassed wisdom, had asked God for it:

> *"So give Your servant an understanding heart to judge Your people to discern between good and evil. For who is able to judge this great people of Yours?"*
>
> *It was pleasing in the sight of the Lord that Solomon had asked this thing. God said to him, "Because you have asked this thing and have not asked for yourself long life, nor have asked riches for yourself, nor have you asked for the life of*

your enemies, but have asked for yourself discernment to understand justice, behold, I have done according to your words. Behold, I have given you a wise and discerning heart, so that there has been no one like you before you, nor shall one like you arise after you (1 KINGS 3:9–12).

How can we make our requests to God for wisdom? Well, in the simplest of terms. We simply admit, "God, I lack wisdom." And then we acknowledge, "But You have a limitless supply of wisdom and you have shown Your desire to share it with the people You have created. You have come to us as Jesus, who is wisdom itself. I ask You to release Your wisdom to me concerning the problem in front of me." And then expect God's wisdom to rise up in you. You may not have to wait long!

Ask with complete faith that God wants to answer your prayer, and He will. That is what James wrote:

But if any of you lacks wisdom, let him ask of God, who gives to all generously and without reproach, and it will be given to him. But he must ask in faith without any doubting, for the one who doubts is like the surf of the sea, driven and tossed by the wind (JAMES 1:5–6).

WHAT IS WISDOM?

Wisdom is so important to God that altogether the words "wisdom" or "wise" are used more than four hundred and fifty-six times in the Bible. Clearly wisdom is a valuable commodity!

Yet do we even understand what wisdom is, or do we just presume we know already? Wise James again provides some idea of what God's wisdom consists of:

The wisdom that comes from heaven is first of all pure and full of quiet gentleness. Then it is peace-loving and courteous. It allows discussion and is willing to yield to others; it is full of mercy and good deeds. It is wholehearted and straightforward and sincere (JAMES 3:17, TLB).

Synonyms for the word "wisdom" help flesh out its meaning. They include: understanding, knowledge, good sense, insight, perception, astuteness, acumen, prudence, sagacity, good judgment, and more. I want and need multiplied quantities of every one of those qualities. How about you?

Some believers in every generation exemplify wisdom to a high degree. In everything they say and do you can recognize the mind and heart of God. Their character is sterling. They care about others more than themselves. They humbly seek God before they give advice or take action. Like anybody, they can veer off the narrow way (Solomon did), but the good fruit of their lives far outweighs the bad.

Wisdom is invaluable for any believer alongside any of the gifts of the Spirit, but in this book I want to highlight its importance to the exercise of the prophetic gift. I do not need to tell you that you and I need all the wisdom we can get, particularly when we are handling a word of revelation.

WISDOM LESSONS—WHAT **NOT** TO DO

Through my many years of active ministry, I have learned a few things. As a prophetic person who was wired to be extra-sensitive, I have needed to keep certain hard-learned lessons in mind. Here are four wisdom lessons that have kept me from floundering; essentially, these are things to avoid.

1. Do not let your "calling" become more important than love. Prophetic revelation can be a pretty heady thing. It can be too easy to misplace your identity and to put it in your gift and calling. My "prophetic papa," Bob Jones, shared an experience in which he found himself in Heaven along with a number of recently deceased individuals. Some of them had made a name for themselves while they were alive, even in the Church, but none of that seemed to count with the Lord, who was questioning each person in turn, "Did you learn to love?" Love is greater than any revelation or exploit. It is more important than the heavenly streets of gold or choirs of angels. Are you learning to love?

We must always take to heart these words of Paul: "Let love be your highest goal! But you should also desire the special abilities the Spirit gives—especially the ability to prophesy" (1 Cor. 14:1, NLT). There was a time in my life when I was so enamored with anything prophetic that I only paid attention to the last part of that verse. Somehow the "love" exhortation was blocked from my field of vision. This was not the case for one of my best mentors, Mahesh Chavda, whose first book was titled, *Only Love Can Make a Miracle*. Nor was it the case for Oral Roberts, who in his extreme old age bestowed this gem of wisdom on my son (who had asked him how to obtain greater effectiveness in praying for healing): "Young man," he said, "if you want to see the sick healed, you've got to learn to love the sick."

2. Do not "disclose Noah's nakedness." Do not be too startled by that statement. What I mean is this: In the story we read in Genesis 9, Noah was lying drunk and naked inside his tent. One of his sons saw him that way and informed the other two sons. Those two sons were wiser than the first one; they walked backward with a garment between them to cover the shame of their father's nakedness, without looking at him as they did so.

Here is how that applies to us. God sometimes reveals to prophets shameful things about other people. These things about other people would bring them into disrepute if they were known at large. In situations like these, a prophet needs to learn the wisdom of holding his or her tongue. It is far better to preserve a sinner's honor than it is to bring them into shame and disgrace. God can still convict the sinner and He can still do His work of restoration, even if nothing has been said in public. "Walk backward" in disclosing the word to the person it applies to. One way of applying this advice: make every effort to forget the word after you finish delivering it.

Early in my ministry I learned this lesson the hard way. There was a particular leader in the church who experienced a moral failure. It had a negative impact on hundreds of people's lives and it resulted in a lot of disillusionment and disappointment. I was asked by a leadership team (and I quite possibly accepted over-eagerly) to be the one who would phone scores of leaders across the country to inform them of this gentleman's moral failure and to let them know that he was being removed from ministry for a year. An uproar resulted. Some people accused me of being judgmental, critical, or of being influenced by a religious spirit. Many wanted to know more than they had to know. I was accused of not walking the tightrope of wisdom and honor and of becoming a talebearer to others. Needless to say, this created a lot of pain in me and it produced a lot of misunderstanding that I could not clear up without making things worse. A number of leaders ended up not trusting me for months or even years. I got put into the "doghouse" for another man's moral failure. It appeared that I had exposed my brother's nakedness, and my actions drove a wedge between us. After a good deal of time, much prayer, and learning some hard lessons in wisdom, the two of us reconciled, but not before we all had suffered a great deal of needless emotional pain.

3. Do not catapult yourself beyond the limits of your sphere. The apostle Paul sagely offered this advice to the Corinthian Christians. He told them (and us) not to boast of authority that we do not possess (see 2 Cor. 10:13–16).[1] This is often referred to as your "sphere of rule" or your *metron*.[2] I have found out about this reality from personal experience. I definitely do not function in the same level of revelation or with the same level of authority everywhere I go. I have had to learn to discern which places I am called to build or bless and which places I am not. I cannot improve my effectiveness in the places I am not called to affect.

Once years ago when I became deeply involved in a major international prophetic controversy, I needed to learn wisdom regarding what He had assigned to me within my sphere of grace and what lay outside of it. I could see that difficulties were brewing and I had a pretty good level of discernment about what to do. Twice I helped bring two leadership teams together and both times I helped to broker an apparent peace. Things were calm for a while, but then they all fell apart. Even my personal call to be a Kingdom peacemaker and bridge-builder and reconciler was not adequate because I had overstepped my sphere of authority. In my eagerness to help, I did not do the right things and I may even have done harm. Take it from me, that is a lesson you do not want to learn firsthand!

4. Do not be confused concerning your sensitive nature. This one may not apply to everyone, but it is certainly one of the wisdom lessons I had to learn. Every prophetic person is wired differently. In my case, God, life, family, and calling have shaped me to be extra-sensitive. This in turn can make me more susceptible to issues of rejection (as discussed in Chapter 6). I have had to learn the wisdom of ways of handling this sensitivity without cursing my gift or wishing I had been wired otherwise. At times the enemy has sown confusion in my mind and conflict in my emotions. I have had to learn how to sort out all of the input and how to consider my makeup a blessing so that I can continue to be a blessing to others.

For example, a sensitive prophet may feel that something is more urgent than it really is. Speaking out or acting too soon may create problems that would not have occurred if the prophet had waited for God's timing for a message and instructions about its method of delivery. Sometimes sensitive prophets can be overcome with tears of travail, which will not help them communicate clearly and may mislead people, and the wisest course of action is to withdraw to another room for a time.

"The spirits of prophets are subject to prophets" (1 Cor. 14:32), so it should always be possible to hold back even strong emotional, prophetic responses.

WISDOM LESSONS—WHAT TO DO

I do not want to make it seem as though the greater part of wisdom consists of cautionary warnings. Here are four more points to balance out the previous ones, and they are all positive:

1. Cultivate a culture of honor. Romans 12:10 reminds us: "Be devoted to one another in brotherly love; give preference to one another in honor." Another way of saying the same thing is "cultivate a culture of honor." This does not mean you have to praise everybody for everything, including those who are not righteous, but it does obligate you to respect the authority and gifts of others in the Church and to refrain from criticism.

It troubles me the way so many prophetic people just do not like the Church. Whether that comes from their history of sensitivity and rejection or something else, it moves them into a critical, antagonistic spirit. They do not seem to realize that their behavior aligns them with the accuser of the brethren. Look at Jesus—He lay down His life for the Church, and He wants us to do the same. The greatest person in our midst is, like Jesus, the servant of all. I want to be one of those servant-of-all people, don't you?

2. Cultivate a relationship with the written and the Living Word. I like to repeat this phrase, which is loaded with wisdom: "Be more impressed with the Word going into you than the word coming out of you." Study to show yourself approved as a workman for God (see 2 Tim. 2:15). Read the Word daily. Listen to it. Memorize it. Speak it out loud. Sing it. Never let a gift of God displace your personal relationship with the Living Word (the person of Jesus) and the living written Word (the Scriptures).

3. Cultivate an awareness of the fact that we are better together. We need each other; two are better than one (see Eccl. 4:9–12).[3] One can chase a thousand to flight, but two can chase ten thousand (see Deut. 32:30).[4] Prophets cannot stand solo. They need pastors and apostles. They need administrators and encouragers. This comes home to us most clearly when we lose someone we have come to rely on, either to death or because they had to move away. They leave a big hole! Isaiah reminds us that "the new wine is found in the cluster" (Isa. 65:8). You cannot expect to make new wine out of just one grape, can you?

4. *Cultivate an adventurous spirit.* Have you ever been a part of a movement of the Holy Spirit? Did excesses occur? Did they put you off, and put others off? Such things always happen, and too many prophetic people become overly cautious and self-protective as a result. They end up sitting out the moves of the Spirit, even becoming judgmental and critical. When the next wave of the Spirit comes along, they take a guarded "wait and see" attitude, and they miss a lot as a result.

So I say—be adventurous! Catch, survive, and thrive in every wave of the Spirit. Take some risks, in faith. The prophetic life is about taking new territory for the Kingdom. Sure, it can get messy. But that is what you signed up for, whether you knew it or not. Keep a clean slate by forgiving the past missteps of others and start afresh, gaining more wisdom lessons as you move forward. You might even find out that it can be a lot of fun!

Wisdom in Journaling

Journaling is simply taking personal notes for future reference. The act of writing something down helps us retain it. Recording revelatory words in a notebook or online document helps prophetic people keep track of the unrecorded revelation they have received.

You had a dream and you have not yet figured out what it means? Write it down. Then you will not forget the details before you have had a chance to meditate on it with God's help. You had a fleeting sense that you should pray for someone and you did? Write it down. You may discover later that your sense of timing was perfect.

Your journaling will be different from mine. You may use a notebook and a pen, or your laptop. You may write down your prayers—and record

God's answers as you perceive them. You may keep a record of what you sense the Holy Spirit is saying to you through His various delivery systems.

I advocate journaling as a naturally supernatural tool for retaining revelation. It is a tried and tested practice that has been used for centuries by believers; it is a fundamental and useful biblical discipline. Journaling will help you understand the revelation you receive from God. And it will help you understand your prophetic self, not to mention the One who reveals things to you.

We see plenty of biblical precedent for writing down the word of the Lord in order to keep track of it. (Actually, you could say that the Bible as a whole is something like a collection of inspired journals of various types.) God instructed Habakkuk to record his vision in writing:

> *Write down the revelation and make it plain on tablets so that a herald may run with it. For the revelation awaits an appointed time; it speaks of the end and will not prove false. Though it linger, wait for it; it will certainly come and will not delay* (HAB. 2:2–3, NIV).

Early in his time of exile in Babylon, Daniel received a dream and visions: "In the first year of Belshazzar king of Babylon, Daniel had a dream, and visions passed through his mind as he was lying in bed. He wrote down the substance of his dream" (Dan. 7:1, NIV).

When you want to write down your own dreams or visions, be careful not to get lost in the details. Write down the basic framework without spending much time trying to interpret it. That account will be enough to remind you of possibly symbolic details later.

Your journals will remind you of significant promises from God that you have received prophetically. In 2004 I was scheduled to teach a class about maturing in the prophetic at the Wagner Leadership Institute. I felt led by the Spirit to include one lesson on journaling, so in preparation I reached into the drawer in my bedroom where I kept my many journals and just pulled some of them out. At the time of the class, I simply picked out of one my journals and I randomly opened it up to read to the class as a personal example. On the page I turned to I found a word from a dream I had recorded that I had totally forgotten about. The page read, "When you are seventy years old, the true apostolic will be in full maturation." At the time, I was fifty-two years old, and seventy seemed far in the future. In fact, I hung on to that word tightly for the next nine years as I went through cancer and many other trials; sometimes I wondered if I would even make it to the next year. As the years have rolled by, I have kept that in mind as a promise from God. Now seventy is only a few years away, and I am very much looking forward to seeing with my own eyes the apostolic in full maturation. What a promise!

An even more personal experience occurred a couple years after my dear wife passed away. I was with the Lord in prayer and He spoke these words to my spirit: "I have a surprise for you today. There is a treasure waiting for you. Look in the top drawer of Ann's nightstand." I had not ever opened the drawer of her nightstand.

When I opened it, I found her journals from years before, when she'd had nine straight weeks of angelic visitations. Those scribbles from when Michal Ann was visited by angels from midnight to 5:00 a.m. every night for nine straight weeks are part of my inheritance now. What a treasure! Someday I will share them with my kids as part of their legacy from their mom.

An Invitation to Step Into the Wisdom Ways of God

If you are called to have a prophetic ministry on any level, you will need to grow in the spirit of wisdom, to increase in wisdom as Jesus did. His heavenly wisdom is available to you simply for the asking. Start asking in faith now. I can assure you that you are in very good company as you step out and pray.

LET'S PRAY

Father, we admit that we lack wisdom, but we also declare that You are generous and that You have a vast and generous supply of wisdom for every person who calls on You. Therefore, we ask for our portion of today's wisdom. You have given each one of us various assignments today, and we cannot accomplish them at all without Your help and wisdom. We want to grow in wisdom daily, as Jesus did. We want to walk out prophetic solutions to complex problems, as Solomon did. We look forward to the increase of both wisdom and revelation that You will release to us. In the holy, great name of Jesus, Amen and Amen!

CHAPTER 12

A LOOK INTO THE FUTURE:
A VISION OF THE BRIDE OF CHRIST

*Christ also loved the church and gave Himself up for her,
so that He might sanctify her, having cleansed her by the
washing of water with the word, that He might present to
Himself the church in all her glory, having no spot or wrinkle
or any such thing; but that she would be holy and blameless.*

EPHESIANS 5:25–27

As part of our prophetic commissioning, we must look not only to our past, asking God to clean us up, heal us, and give us boldness and wisdom, but we must also look to the future...way into the future. Not to tomorrow or next year, but to the end of the church age, when our Lord Jesus Christ will present the Church as a Bride to Himself.

We can find a vision of the completed Bride of Christ in Ezekiel's account of what happened in the valley of dry bones. It is a story of restoration with two parts: first the natural restoration of the physical bodies that had been nothing more than disarticulated skeletons and second, the restoration of the breath of life to each of the individuals who had been raised up, so that they could become a living army, assembled for action:

The Lord took hold of me, and I was carried away by the Spirit of the Lord to a valley filled with bones. He led me all around among the bones that covered the valley floor. They were scattered everywhere across the ground and were completely dried out. Then he asked me, "Son of man, can these bones become living people again?"

"O Sovereign Lord," I replied, "you alone know the answer to that."

Then he said to me, "Speak a prophetic message to these bones and say, 'Dry bones, listen to the word of the Lord! This is what the Sovereign Lord says: Look! I am going to put breath into you and make you live again! I will put flesh and muscles on you and cover you with skin. I will put breath into you, and you will come to life. Then you will know that I am the Lord.'"

So I spoke this message, just as he told me. Suddenly as I spoke, there was a rattling noise all across the valley. The bones of each body came together and attached themselves as complete skeletons. Then as I watched, muscles and flesh formed over the bones. Then skin formed to cover their bodies, but they still had no breath in them.

Then he said to me, "Speak a prophetic message to the winds, son of man. Speak a prophetic message and say, 'This is what the Sovereign Lord says: Come, O breath, from the four winds! Breathe into these dead bodies so they may live again.'"

So I spoke the message as he commanded me, and breath came into their bodies. They all came to life and stood up on their feet—a great army.

Then he said to me, "Son of man, these bones represent the people of Israel. They are saying, 'We have become old, dry bones—all hope is gone. Our nation is finished.' Therefore, prophesy to them and say, 'This is what the Sovereign Lord says: O my people, I will open your graves of exile and cause you to rise again. Then I will bring you back to the land of Israel. When this happens, O my people, you will know that I am the Lord. I will put my Spirit in you, and you will live again and return home to your own land. Then you will know that I, the Lord, have spoken, and I have done what I said. Yes, the Lord has spoken!'" (EZEK. 37:1–14, NLT)

The spiritual restoration follows the natural restoration.[1] When God took Ezekiel to the valley of dry bones in a vision and asked him the question, "Son of man, can these bones become living people again?" Ezekiel did not know the answer. Then God spoke a prophetic solution to the current situation, which changed the situation drastically. Ezekiel was instructed to prophesy life to the bones—which is a direct parallel to what we as prophetic people have been instructed by God to do for the current generation. Just as Ezekiel was commissioned to prophesy life to the fragmented bodies of the army of warriors, so we have been commissioned to prophesy life to the broken Body of Christ. We have been called to prophesy life to the dried-out structures of the Church and we have been called to prophesy new life to those who have been destined to become part of it. After that we have been told to turn and prophesy life to the wind, inviting the breath of the Holy Spirit—the *ruach*,[2] the *pneuma*[3]—to come in and enter the Body of Christ in our sphere of influence, so that the Body can be further perfected as the Bride of Christ. (The New Testament never uses the term "Bride of Christ," but Ephesians 5 comes close when it compares a husband's care for his wife to Christ's care for the church body.)

At the Creation, God created Adam's body first, but it was not until He breathed His spirit mouth to mouth into his body that Adam became a living, moving being. He was already well-formed by his Maker in his body, but that did not mean a thing until he came alive as a "living soul" (see Gen. 2:7). In preparation for the birth of the Church on the day of Pentecost (see Acts 2), Jesus breathed His Spirit into the group of His disciples who would become its shepherds saying, "Receive the Holy Spirit" (John 20:22).

At the present time, we exist in a state of ongoing restoration. We reach out to others, echoing the words of Peter on the Day of Pentecost:

> *Repent therefore and be converted, that your sins may be blotted out, so that times of refreshing may come from the presence of the Lord, and that He may send Jesus Christ, who was preached to you before, whom heaven must receive until the times of restoration of all things, which God has spoken by the mouth of all His holy prophets since the world began* (ACTS 3:19–21, NKJV).

When will the second coming of Jesus happen? He will not come until the period of the restoration is complete of all things that pertain to His Church. Then He will claim His long-awaited Bride. The prophetic task of His people is a big one, and only by following Him together obediently can we accomplish a full restoration of His message and methods. First prophetic people (such as you and I) must volunteer to carry His message to every hidden nook and cranny of every region of the earth. Our message is the Gospel of the Kingdom of God. It is not only the Good News of salvation for individuals, but also the Good News of healing, deliverance, and salvation in every dimension, meant for everyone who has ears to hear. A unified army of restored men and women must arise from the dispersed dry bones.

The messengers are not only the evangelists and pastors but also the apostles, prophets, and teachers—those who carry the five representative ministry gifts that are listed by the apostle Paul in Ephesians:

And He gave some as apostles, and some as prophets, and some as evangelists, and some as pastors and teachers, for the equipping of the saints for the work of service, to the building up of the body of Christ; until we all attain to the unity of the faith, and of the knowledge of the Son of God, to a mature man, to the measure of the stature which belongs to the fullness of Christ (Eph. 4:11–13).

Alongside the restoration of the message and the messengers will come a restoration of the biblical methods of both communicating and activating the message. "'Not by might nor by power, but by My Spirit,' says the Lord of hosts" (see Zech. 4:6). The spiritual gifts such as the gift of prophecy have been given for the purposes of serving and equipping the saints, for continually building up the Body of Christ, with the end in view.

The gifts of the Spirit have been given to every generation of believers so that every generation can do its part to bring about the attainment of "the unity of the faith," "the knowledge of the Son of God"—the maturity in the full stature and maturity of Christ. This remains the task to which we have been called, with each one of us contributing his or her part. To this day, we are operating in a pattern of the restoration of all things.

Parallel and Progressive Moves of the Holy Spirit

We have not yet "arrived," have we? Yet in the pattern of Ezekiel 37, we have seen an amazing physical restoration in the rebirth of the nation of Israel in 1948. This is, in my opinion, the greatest fulfillment of Bible prophecy that has happened in recent Church history. God's chosen people, the Jews, who had been scattered across the world for over two thousand years, but who had kept their language and culture incredibly intact, were allowed, against all odds, to resettle their ancestral homeland. This is a definite physical restoration, and it raises our expectations for a parallel spiritual restoration, not only for the Jewish people but also for the Church.

The Church, the Body of Christ, remains dispersed and to some extent on its last legs. And yet this situation is no more hopeless than Ezekiel's dead bones or the diaspora of the Jews, because it is possible to trace wave after wave of progress. I am not a trained church historian, but from where I sit I can see at least a dozen progressive movements of the Spirit in the past two hundred years or so, and they have not faltered up to the present day. (If anything, they have accelerated.) Through the following movements, the Church has been changed, never to go back to its previous condition:

1. the Holiness movement

2. the Pentecostal movement

3. the signs and wonders movement

4. the Latter Rain movement

5. the healing and deliverance movement

6. the evangelical movement

7. the charismatic movement

8. the Jesus People movement

9. the Messianic movement

10. the prayer movement

11. the Third Wave movement

12. the prophetic movement

We are in the midst of yet another wave—a global worship and prayer movement. I can tell you from my own life experience that a little over twenty-five years ago almost nobody had ever heard of a "house of prayer."

There may have been about eight of them total in all of North America. Within a span of only ten years, this number grew until there were over ten thousand houses of prayer, and it is quite possible that the worship and prayer movement has not yet reached its crescendo.

Building on earlier movements, the late C. Peter Wagner contributed directly to the worship and prayer movement as well as many others by assembling leaders from disparate parts of the Body of Christ so that they could connect with each other and find out what God had for them to do together. He identified contemporary movements of the Spirit by giving them names or by highlighting and resurrecting names that had fallen into disuse.

Another way of talking about these various movements past and present is to call them "revivals." Any of us who have been around for a while will have been touched by a few of them, and we know that often they have been what you might call "centric," that is, centered in a particular geographic region such as Wales or Los Angeles or Seoul or Kansas City or Toronto. If a revival was not happening in your local area, you had to travel to it if you wanted to be part of it personally. I believe that as the Spirit keeps working across the face of the earth, there are going to be apostolic hubs in every major city. Even though it is only in the beginning stages, I can envision it, and I want to be around long enough to see it in its fullness with my own eyes.

These various movements of the Holy Spirit have influenced each other and have overlapped. Sometimes they have been known by different names. But the point I am making here is a straightforward one, namely that the Holy Spirit has been at work restoring the Church, the Body of Christ, so that she can become His spotlessly perfect Bride.

Again, without claiming for myself the title of modern church historian, I have been both a participant and an observer in several additional movements of the Spirit since the turn of the millennium in the year 2000.

I distinguish the following patterns and movements, all of which are leading up to a glorious culmination under the lordship of Jesus Christ:

1. the worship and presence of God movement (see Rev. 5:11–14)

2. the second apostolic movement (see Acts 3:19–21)

3. the "all saints" movement (see Eph. 4:11–12)[4]

4. the global harvest movement (see Luke 10:2)[5]

5. the "glory of the Lord poured out" (see Isa. 60:1–2)[6]

6. a final great harvest (see Joel 3:13)[7]

7. the second coming of the Lord Jesus Christ (see Rev. 19:11–16)

8. the complete restoration of the Kingdom of God: "Thy Kingdom come on earth" (see Rev. 21:1)

The model prayer of Jesus is being answered. He prayed, "Thy Kingdom come on earth as it is in heaven" (see Matt. 6:10) and that prayer has to mean that the glory of the Lord will truly cover the face of the earth as the waters cover the sea. "…For the earth will be filled with the knowledge of the glory of the Lord as the waters cover the sea" (Hab. 2:14, NIV; see also Isa. 11:9).

You and I are privileged to be part of what I call the "Greater Works Generation"; that name comes from the wording of John 14:12: "Truly, truly, I say to you, he who believes in Me, the works that I do, he will do also; and greater works than these he will do; because I go to the Father."

Every promise that He has made to you will be fulfilled whether, like me, you have cheated death multiple times, or whether your path has seemed smooth and free from threats. I know why I am still alive—I live to see the fullness of His promises to me. So do you.

All things are possible by faith, and every believer in Christ Jesus can step into greater and greater works, particularly when they are united with other believers in the Church and filled to overflowing with the Spirit of God. To some this level of expectation will seem like a fantasy, but it could not be truer. The Kingdom is coming, and we have tasted it. I can only speak for myself when I say I simply cannot get enough of it!

A Glorious Eschatology

This is a glorious eschatology, a glory-filled, joy-filled expectancy for the time to come! When you take all of the prophetic promises in Scripture and combine them with their fulfillment that continues to be worked out before our very eyes, you know for a fact that the darkness and confusion around us is temporary. Isaiah's words could not be more motivating and trustworthy:

> *Arise, shine; for your light has come, and the glory of the Lord has risen upon you. For behold, darkness will cover the earth and deep darkness the peoples; but the Lord will rise upon you and His glory will appear upon you. Nations will come to your light, and kings to the brightness of your rising* (Isa. 60:1–3).

Everything that I have been teaching and proclaiming in this book comes straight from the Bible; I have not added anything that Scripture does not say. I have not lowered my expectations to match the darkness or the very real difficulties in my experience of the present condition of the world. No, instead I have tried to lay out the conditions we must meet in order to unlock our prophetic potential so that we can prophesy life wherever we go. Our families, our churches, our cities, and our nations need our help to receive their prophetic destiny in the Kingdom of God.

As we move from our training grounds into being God's "sent ones," we will be launched like the eagles of God. This generation will soar farther and higher than ever before, using Heaven-sent keen insights to confront the enemies of the Kingdom while reproducing more eagles who are fiercer and increasingly better at what they do. Together with each other and with our Holy Spirit as guide, we will surround every sphere of society. Some of us will be sent out quite literally, as Saul and Barnabas were sent out from Antioch (see Acts 13:1–3),[8] while others will quietly labor behind the scenes in prayer and obedient service. No one will be left behind. Fueled by God's inexhaustible supply of fiery love and vibrant life, we will not stop until He tells us to.

Where are we in God's timetable? No one can say for sure. But I know one thing: We are closer than we ever were before to the grand finale. Jesus is coming back for His Bride and—get this—*He will not allow Himself to be unequally yoked.* Hard as it may be to imagine, His Bride/Church will be spotless and without blemish in that day.

> *Hallelujah!*
> *For our Lord God Almighty reigns.*
> *Let us rejoice and be glad*
> *and give him glory!*
> *For the wedding of the Lamb has come,*
> *and his bride has made herself ready* (REV. 19:6–7, NIV).

Saints of God, dear prophetic pilgrims, are you with me in this? We must ask the question, "How would Jesus express being a prophet in today's times and society? We must learn from the past while listening for His reply and do what He desires.

So I ask in closing, "Do you want to be a part of creating and sustaining a culture of life in the prophetic today?" If so, let's keep our hand to the plow and keep looking straight ahead at Jesus! He is our aim. He is our goal.

LET'S PRAY

Father, in Jesus' wonderful name, we declare that the best is yet to come. We proclaim that the best wine is being saved until the end. We rejoice as we gaze into the eyes of our Beloved, fully convinced that He has a wonderful plan, purpose, and destiny for us—because we belong to His Church and He is making us into a Bride fit for a King. Here at the convergence of the ages, we see that the fields are ripe for the harvest. We ask You to pour out Your Spirit upon all mankind and let Your Son Jesus receive the rewards for His suffering. Amen, Amen, Amen!

SCRIPTURES ABOUT PROPHECY

PROPHECY IN THE OLD TESTAMENT

Genesis 5:29
Genesis 22:7–8
Genesis 27:28–29
Genesis 27:39–40
Genesis 48:13–20
Genesis 49:1–27

Exodus 15:14–18
Exodus 16:6–7

Leviticus 9:6

Numbers 11:24–39
Numbers 13:30
Numbers 14:6–9
Numbers 23:7–10
Numbers 23:18–24
Numbers 24:1–9
Numbers 24:15–24

Deuteronomy 32:1–47

Deuteronomy 33:1–29

Joshua 10:25
Joshua 24:1–14

Judges 6:8–10

1 Samuel 2:1–10
1 Samuel 24:1–14

2 Samuel 3:18–19
2 Samuel 7:8–17
2 Samuel 23:1–7

2 Kings 3:15–18

1 Chronicles 17:4–15
1 Chronicles 22:8–13
1 Chronicles 22:17–19

2 Chronicles 15:2–7
2 Chronicles 20:17–19

Ezra 9:6-15

Nehemiah 2:20
Nehemiah 9:6–37

Psalm 89:19–37

Isaiah 1:18–20
Isaiah 12:1–6
Isaiah 25:6–12
Isaiah 26:1–21
Isaiah 29:17–24
Isaiah 35:1–10
Isaiah 44:1–5
Isaiah 44:6–8
Isaiah 55:1–13
Isaiah 56:1–8
Isaiah 60:1–9
Isaiah 60:10–14
Isaiah 60:15–22

Ezekiel 11:16
Ezekiel 11:17–20
Ezekiel 28:25–26
Ezekiel 34:11–16
Ezekiel 34:24–31

Hosea 2:14–20
Hosea 6:1–3
Hosea 11:8–9

Hosea 14:1–7

Joel 2:12–14
Joel 3:18–21

Amos 9:13–15

Obadiah v.17

Micah 2:12–13
Micah 4:1–5
Micah 4:6–8
Micah 7:18–20

Nahum 2:2

Habakkuk 2:14

Zephaniah 2:7
Zephaniah 3:14–20

Haggai 2:5–9
Haggai 2:23

Zechariah 8:7–13
Zechariah 8:14–17
Zechariah 10:1
Zechariah 10:6–12

Malachi 1:11
Malachi 3:16–18
Malachi 4:1–6

PROPHECY IN THE NEW TESTAMENT

Mark 10:30
Mark 14:8–9

Luke 1:41–45
Luke 1:46–55

Luke 1:67–80
Luke 2:25–32
Luke 2:33–35
Luke 22:31–32

John 6:31–35

Acts 1:4–8
Acts 2:14–37
Acts 11:28
Acts 13:1–3
Acts 15:30–35
Acts 20:28–31
Acts 21:10–11

Ephesians 1:17–23

Revelation 2:1–7
Revelation 2:8–11
Revelation 2:12–17
Revelation 2:18–29
Revelation 3:1–6
Revelation 3:7–13
Revelation 3:14–22

TRYING TO PROPHESY?

Here is some practical advice for getting started:

1. Earnestly desire the gifts of the Holy Spirit, especially that you may prophesy (see 1 Cor. 14:1). God wants to speak to you and through you!

2. Trust the peace of God. Beware of speaking when your spirit is uneasy or in turmoil, or when you feel forced to speak. Look for the peace of God in every word you utter (see Ps. 85:8; Phil. 4:7–9).

3. Obey the urging of the Spirit. Remember, the prophetic spirit is under your control. It will not impel you to speak against your better judgment. You can turn it off or turn it on by an act of your will.

4. Don't rely on physical sensations. When you begin to move in prophecy the Lord may give you physical sensations such as knots in the stomach, a fluttering heartbeat, intense heat, a feeling of euphoria, impressions, visions, and so on. The Holy Spirit does this to prepare you to receive or deliver His word. However, it is also true that as time goes on, the Lord often withholds these promptings so you can grow in the ability to hear Him apart from physical sensations.

5. Speak clearly and naturally. You don't have to speak in King James English to get your point across. Nor do you always have to say, "Thus saith the Lord." If your word is truly from God, the Spirit will confirm it in the hearts of the listeners (see John 10:4–5, 16). Also, be sure to speak loudly and clearly enough to be heard by everyone.

6. Timing is everything. A prophecy that comes at the wrong time during a meeting sounds like a noisy gong or clanging symbol. It will only draw attention to you, not to Jesus.

7. Leave the delivery of corrective and directional words to experienced and mature brothers and sisters. The simple gift of prophecy is for exhortation, edification, and comfort. If you do receive a directional word, write it down and prayerfully submit it to someone in leadership for evaluation.

8. How do you receive a message? You don't have to be struck by a lightning bolt to prophesy. A message can come in a variety of ways: literal words; senses or inklings; vision of words like teletype print in your mind; dreams; and so on. More often than not, a seasoned individual receives the sense of what God wants to say. Your duty is to then express that sense clearly and appropriately (see Ps. 12:6).

9. What do you do with a word after you've received it? That depends. Not all words are for the purpose of proclamation; many are for intercession. Some words should be "put on file," waiting for confirmation. Other words should be written down and submitted to more mature Christians with a prophetic ministry for evaluation. Some prophecies should only be spoken to an individual, others to a group. Some prophetic words should be delivered as songs.

10. What if you mess up? No start is perfect. Maturity only comes from taking risks and occasionally failing. Proverbs 24:16 says, "For a righteous man falls seven times and rises again." Learn from your mistakes, ask the Lord to forgive and cleanse you, and get back up and humbly receive His grace (see 1 Pet. 5:5).

PRACTICAL SUGGESTIONS FOR PRESENTING AND ADMINISTRATING PROPHECY IN CORPORATE SETTINGS

(Adapted in part from Mike Bickle's book, *Growing in the Prophetic*)

1. *Make sure that your heart is open* to receiving words from the Lord.

2. Remember the *three distinct components of presenting prophecy:* revelation, interpretation, and application. You must discern all three components with wisdom. Remember also that the Lord will often use three different people to put these parts together.

3. Leaders, be sure to *communicate verbally and in print* to inform newcomers of your guidelines and ground rules regarding the giving and receiving of prophecy in your fellowship.

4. Leaders, God may not speak to you as directly as those with a prophetic anointing, but He will speak to you and give you

His perspective if you ask Him. *Don't be intimidated* by the prophetic gifting of others. You have been divinely appointed to judge and discern the claims of divine inspirations and your concern must be for the overall good of the flock.

5. Leaders, deal humbly and frankly with people whose prophesying is not edifying others in either its content or presentation. *Give them specific practical boundaries* based on their prophetic maturity as far as you can determine it. Be sure to communicate any changes that develop as they grow.

6. Leaders, *appeal to those prophetically anointed to be more "normal"* and to not take themselves so seriously. Encourage them to be open to correction and adjustment and to offer their words in a humble style (with less melodrama and in the common vernacular!). Remind them that the Lord does not need their help or their hype to perform His word, and that it is better for them to try to be less "heroic" and more helpful to other believers.

7. Leaders, *don't be afraid to withhold the microphone.* It is all right simply to say "no." It is good for those with prophetic anointing to be tested in patience and in their trust in the Lord regarding the delivery of prophetic words. This is especially true for dramatic words of knowledge. "Someone here has a headache" is very different from, "A man named Thomas, who is sitting over there, was diagnosed yesterday as having lymphatic cancer."

8. Leaders should *have the integrity and humility to "mop up" any messes* that are caused by wrong prophecies or their poor administration. This is the only way to ensure that your congregation's "corporate conscience" stays clear regarding the gift of prophecy.

FOR FURTHER READING

(Many of these titles are out of print,
but most are still available from booksellers.)

Austin, Dorothea. *The Name Book*. Minneapolis: Bethany, 1982.

Blomgren, David. *Prophetic Gatherings in the Church: The Laying on of Hands and Prophecy*. Portland, Ore.: Bible Temple, 1979.

——. Song of the Lord. Portland, Ore.: Bible Temple, 1978. Breathitt, Barbie. *The Gateway to the Seer Realm*. Shippensburg, Penn.: Destiny Image, 2012.

Bullinger, Ethelbert W. *Number in Scripture: Its Supernatural Design and Spiritual Significance*. Grand Rapids: Kregel, 1967.

Castro, David A. *Understanding Supernatural Dreams According to the Bible*. Brooklyn: Anointed Publications, 1994.

Chevreau, Guy. *Pray with Fire: Interceding in the Spirit*. Toronto: Harper-Perennial/HarperCollins, 1995.

Conner, Kevin J. *Interpreting the Symbols and Types*. Portland, Ore.: City Christian Publishing, 1980.

Conner, Kevin J., and Ken Malmin. *Interpreting the Scriptures*. Portland, Ore.: City Christian Publishing, 1983.

Crist, Terry. *Warring According to Prophecy*. New Kensington, Penn.: Whitaker House, 1989.

Cunningham, Loren. *Is That Really You, God?* Seattle: YWAM, 1984.

Damazio, Frank. *Developing the Prophetic Ministry*. Portland, Ore.: Trilogy Productions, 1983.

Deere, Jack. *Surprised by the Voice of God*. Grand Rapids, MI: Zondervan Publishing House, 1996.

Foster, Glenn. *The Purpose and Use of Prophecy*. Dubuque, Iowa: Kendall Hunt Publishing Co., 1988.

Galloway, Jamie. *Secrets of the Seer*. Shippensburg, Penn.: Destiny Image, 2017.

Grudem, Wayne. *The Gift of Prophecy in the New Testament and Today*. Wheaton, Ill.: Crossway, 1988.

Hagin, Kenneth. *Concerning Spiritual Gifts*. Tulsa: Faith Library. 1976.

——. *The Gift of Prophecy*. Tulsa: Faith Library, 1982.

——. *The Holy Spirit and His Gifts*. Tulsa: Faith Library.

——. *The Ministry of a Prophet*. Tulsa: Faith Library, 1981.

Hamon, Bill. *Prophets and Personal Prophecy: Guidelines for Receiving, Understanding, and Fulfilling God's Personal Word to You*. Shippensburg, Penn.: Destiny Image, 1987.

——. *Prophets and the Prophetic Movement*. Shippensburg, Penn.: Destiny Image, 1990.

——. *Prophets, Pitfalls, and Principles*. Shippensburg, Penn.: Destiny Image, 1991.

Hamon, Jane. *Dreams and Visions*. Grand Rapids, Mich.: Chosen Books, 2016.

Iverson, Dick. *The Holy Spirit Today*. Portland, Ore.: Bible Temple, 1976.

Jacobs, Cindy. *The Voice of God*. Bloomington, MN: Chosen Books, 2016.

Kelsey, Morton T. *God, Dreams, and Revelation*. Minneapolis: Augsburg House, 1974.

LeClaire, Jennifer. *The Making of a Prophet*. Grand Rapids, Mich.: Chosen Books, 2014.

Maloney, James. *The Panoramic Seer*. Shippensburg, Penn.: Destiny Image, 2012.

Mumford, Bob. *Take Another Look at Guidance: Discerning the Will of God*. Plainsfield, N.J.: Logos International, 1971.

Prince, Derek. *How to Judge Prophecy*. Fort Lauderdale, Fla.: Derek Prince, 1971.

Pytches, David. *Prophecy in the Local Church: A Practical Handbook and Historical Overview*. London: Hodder and Stoughton, 1993.

——. *Spiritual Gifts in the Local Church*. Minneapolis: Bethany, 1985.

Riffel, Herman H. *Dream Interpretation: A Biblical Understanding*. Shippensburg: Destiny Image, 1993.

——. *Dreams: Wisdom Within*, Shippensburg, Penn.: Destiny Image, 1989.

Scott, Martin. *Prophecy in the Church*. Lake Mary, Fla.: Charisma House, 1993.

Swope, Mary Ruth. *Listening Prayer*. New Kensington, Penn.: Whitaker House, 1987.

Thomas, Benny. *Exploring the World of Dreams*. New Kensington, Penn.: Whitaker House, 1990.

Tompkins, Iverna and Judson Cornwall, *On the Ash Heap with No Answers*. Lake Mary Fla.: Charisma House, 1992.

Vallotton, Kris. *Basic Training for the Prophetic Ministry*. Shippensburg: Destiny Image, 2014.

Virkler, Mark and Patti. *Communion with God*. Shippensburg, Penn.: Destiny Image, 1990.

——. *Dialogue with God*. Gainesville, Fla.: Bridge-Logos, 1986.

Werner, Ana. *The Seer's Path*. Shippensburg, Penn.: Destiny Image, 2017.

Wilson, Walter. *A Dictionary of Bible Types*. Grand Rapids, Mich.: William B. Eerdmans, 1950.

Yocum, Bruce. *Prophecy*. Ann Arbor, Mich.: Servant, 1976.

NOTES

CHAPTER ONE:

Where Eagles Dare to Fly

1. "Still another said, 'I will follow you, Lord; but first let me go back and say goodbye to my family.' Jesus replied, 'No one who puts a hand to the plow and looks back is fit for service in the kingdom of God'" (Luke 9:61–62, NIV).

2. Andrew Murray, *With Wings as Eagles* (New Kensington, Penn.: Whitaker House, 1993), 63–64.

CHAPTER TWO:

The History of Prophetic Ministry

1. Irenaeus, Philip Schaff, ed., "Against Heresies," *The Ante-Nicene Fathers,* vol. 1, chap. LXXXII (CreateSpace/Eternal Sun Books), 209.

2. Thomas Aquinas, *Summa theologiae* II-II, 174, 6 ad 3.

3. See Thomas M'Crie, *Lives of Scottish Reformers* (Xenia, Ohio: Board of the Calvinistic Book Concern 1846), 137.

Chapter Four:

Receiving and Releasing the Gift of Prophecy

1. W.E. Vine, *Vine's Expository Dictionary of New Testament Words*, entry for "Prophecy, Prophesy, Prophesying," https://www.studylight.org/dictionaries/ved/p/prophecy-prophesy-prophesying.html. 1940.

2. Dick Iverson, *The Holy Spirit Today* (Portland, Ore.: City Christian Publishing, 2006), 159.

3. Derek Prince, *The Gifts of the Spirit* (New Kensington, Penn.: Whitaker House, 2007), 179.

4. Ibid., 183.

5. Scriptural examples include 2 Kings 3:15; 1 Chronicles 25:1–3; Colossians 3:16; and Ephesians 5:19.

6. "Prophetic etiquette" is a term made popular by Michael Sullivant in a book by the same name.

Chapter Six:

The Prophet and the Rejection Syndrome

1. "Can a woman forget her nursing child, and not have compassion on the son of her womb? Surely they may forget, yet I will not forget you. See, I have inscribed you on the palms of My hands" (Isa. 49:15–16, NKJV).

2. See 1 Cor. 12:7; 14:3, 12; Eph. 4:10–16, 2 Tim. 3:16–17; 2 Pet. 1:19–21.

3. You can consult my book, *Deliverance from Darkness* for more on this subject.

CHAPTER SEVEN:

Seven Modes of Prophetic Communication

1. For example, see the introductory verse of the book of the prophet Nahum: "The *oracle* of Nineveh. The book of the vision of Nahum the Elkoshite..." (Nah. 1:1, emphasis added). Also see Numbers 24:2–4, "The Spirit of God came upon him [Balaam]. He took up his discourse and said, 'The *oracle* of Balaam the son of Beor, and the oracle of the man whose eye is opened; the oracle of him who hears the words of God, who sees the vision of the Almighty.'"

2. See also Isa. 1:1–9; Isa. 45:14–17; Isa. 48:17–19; Isa. 49:5–7; Isa. 50:1–3; Isa. 55:1–13; Isa. 56:1–8; Jer. 2:1–3; and Ezek. 34. Possible New Testament examples include Acts 13:1–3; Acts 15:30–35; and Acts 21:10–11.

3. "After these things I looked, and behold, a great multitude which no one could number, of all nations, tribes, peoples, and tongues, standing before the throne and before the Lamb, clothed with white robes, with palm branches in their hands" (Rev. 7:9, NKJV).

4. For more about prophetic prayer, see my book, *Praying with God's Heart: The Power and Purpose of Prophetic Intercession.*

5. What a little gem of a scriptural prayer: "I pray that God, the source of hope, will fill you completely with joy and peace because you trust in him. Then you will overflow with confident hope through the power of the Holy Spirit" (Rom. 15:13, NLT).

6. For more about prophetic song, see my chapter called "The Prophetic Song of the Lord" in the book, *The Lost Art of Pure Worship.*

7. Other examples can be found in Isaiah 5:1–31; Isaiah 26:1–21; Isaiah 27:2–11; Isaiah 42:10–13; Ezekiel 19:1–14; and Ezekiel 27:1–36. Note that a "lamentation," (as in Ezekiel 19 and 27) is a funeral song.

8. For more on this subject, see my book, *The Discerner: Hearing, Confirming, and Acting on Prophetic Revelation.*

9. For more information, refer to my book, *The Seer: The Prophetic Power of Dreams, Visions, and Open Heavens* as well as *Dream Language: The Prophetic Power of Dreams, Revelations, and the Spirit of Wisdom.*

10. Here is a list of references selected from the many Scriptures that refer to prophetic dreams or visions: Gen. 46:2; Num. 24:16; 1 Sam. 1:1; 2 Sam. 7:17; 1 Kings 23:17 (also 2 Chron. 18:16); Jer. 1:11–19; Jer. 24:1–10; Ezek. 1:1–28; Ezek. 8:1–18; Ezek. 9:1–11; Ezek. 10:1–22 7; Ezek. 11:1–13; Ezek. 37:1–11; Ezek. 40:1–49; Ezek. 41–48:35; Dan. 2:19; Dan. 4:1–18; Dan. 7:1–28; Dan. 8:1–27; Amos 1:1ff; Obad. 1:1ff; Micah 1:1ff; Nah. 1:1ff; Hab. 1:1ff; Zech. 1:8ff; Luke 1:22; Luke 24:23; Acts 9:10; Acts 10:1–33; Acts 16:9–13; 2 Cor. 12:1; and the entire book of Revelation.

11. Other Scriptures that describe prophetic action can be found in Jeremiah 13:1–11; Jeremiah 19:1–15; Ezekiel 4:1–17; Ezekiel 24:1–27; and Ezekiel 37:15-23.

12. For more on this subject, see the lesson titled "Prophetic Gestures and Actions" in my *Understanding Supernatural Encounters Study Guide*.

CHAPTER EIGHT:

Prophetic Women

1. Other similarly gifted women were the three daughters of Heman, the king's seer, who also had fourteen sons, and "All these were under the direction of their father for the music in the house of the Lord" (see 1 Chron. 25:5–6).

2. "So, my dear brothers and sisters, be eager to prophesy, and don't forbid speaking in tongues" (1 Cor. 14:39, NLT).

CHAPTER NINE:

Influencing the Seven Spheres of Society

1. (1) The turning of water into wine (John 2:1–12), (2) the healing of the royal official's son (John 4:46–54), (3) the healing of the paralytic at the pool of Bethesda (John 5:1–17), (4) the feeding of the five thousand (John 6:1–14), (5) Jesus walking on water (John 6:15–25), (6) the healing of the

man born blind (John 9:1–41), and (7) the raising of Lazarus from the dead (John 11:1–46).

2. (1) the Parable of the Sower, (2) the Parable of the Tares, (3) the Parable of the Mustard Seed, (4) the Parable of the Leaven, (5) the Parable of the Hidden Treasure, (6) the Parable of the Pearl, and (7) the Parable of Drawing in the Net.

3. Matt. 23:14–36.

4. (1) "Father, forgive them; for they know not what they do"; (2) "Woman, behold your son! ...Behold your mother!"; (3) Luke 23:43, "Truly I say to you, today you shall be with Me in Paradise"; (4) "Eli, Eli, lama sabachthani? My God, my God, why hast thou forsaken me?"; (5) "I thirst"; (6) "Father, into your hands I commit my spirit"; and (7) "It is finished."

5. The best-known teachers of this approach to fulfilling the Great Commission have been Bill Bright, Loren Cunningham, Lance Wallnau, Os Hillman, and Johnny Enlow.

6. "So Joshua fought the Amalekites as Moses had ordered, and Moses, Aaron and Hur went to the top of the hill. As long as Moses held up his hands, the Israelites were winning, but whenever he lowered his hands, the Amalekites were winning. When Moses' hands grew tired, they took a stone and put it under him and he sat on it. Aaron and Hur held his hands up—one on one side, one on the other—so that his hands remained steady till sunset" (Exod. 17:10–12, NIV).

7. "If a son asks for bread from any father among you, will he give him a stone? Or if he asks for a fish, will he give him a serpent instead of a fish?" (Luke 11:11, NKJV).

CHAPTER TEN:

From Surrender to Sent Ones

1. HIM is an apostolic network of churches, ministries, missions organizations, church networks, and marketplace ministers all committed to loving and helping each other fulfill the Great Commission.

2. See "John Paul in Charisma Digital Magazine" on the website, Streams Ministries, Canada (https://streamscanada.com/index .php?page=news&type=news&id=102).

3. "Then the seventy returned with joy, saying, 'Lord, even the demons are subject to us in Your name'" (Luke 10:17, NKJV).

4. "Remember your leaders, who spoke the word of God to you. Consider the outcome of their way of life and imitate their faith" (Heb. 13:7).

5. No one resource can capture every possible hidden biblical symbolism, but one of the best is Kevin J. Connor's book, *Interpreting the Symbols and Types*.

Chapter Eleven:

Learning Ways of Wisdom

1. "We will not boast about things done outside our area of authority. We will boast only about what has happened within the boundaries of the work God has given us, which includes our working with you. We are not reaching beyond these boundaries when we claim authority over you, as if we had never visited you. For we were the first to travel all the way to Corinth with the Good News of Christ. Nor do we boast and claim credit for the work someone else has done. Instead, we hope that your faith will grow so that the boundaries of our work among you will be extended. Then we will be able to go and preach the Good News in other places far beyond you, where no one else is working. Then there will be no question of our boasting about work done in someone else's territory" (2 Cor. 10:13–16, NLT).

2. In biblical Greek, "a measure" or a geographical sphere. See Strong's Exhaustive Concordance #3358.

3. "Two are better than one, because they have a good reward for their labor. For if they fall, one will lift up his companion. But woe to him who is alone when he falls, for he has no one to help him up. Again, if two lie down together, they will keep warm; but how can one be warm alone? Though one

may be overpowered by another, two can withstand him. And a threefold cord is not quickly broken" (Eccl. 4:9–12, NKJV).

4. "How could one person chase a thousand of them, and two people put ten thousand to flight, unless their Rock had sold them, unless the Lord had given them up?" (Deut. 32:30, NLT).

Chapter Twelve:

A Look Into the Future: A Vision of the Bride of Christ

1. "However, the spiritual is not first, but the natural, and afterward the spiritual" (1 Cor. 15:46, NKJV).

2. *Ruach*, Hebrew word meaning "breath, wind, spirit" (Strong's Hebrew Concordance #7307).

3. *Pneuma,* Greet word meaning "life, wind, spirit" (Strong's Greek Concordance #4151).

4. "Some of us have been given special ability as apostles; to others he has given the gift of being able to preach well; some have special ability in winning people to Christ, helping them to trust him as their Savior; still others have a gift for caring for God's people as a shepherd does his sheep, leading and teaching them in the ways of God. Why is it that he gives us these special abilities to do certain things best? It is that God's people will be equipped to do better work for him, building up the Church, the body of Christ, to a position of strength and maturity" (Eph. 4:11–12, TLB)

5. This is not the same as the final great harvest, but I believe that it is the greatest harvest that the Church has ever seen. It will restore many backsliders who will turn and become some of the most effective evangelists to the lost.

6. "Arise, shine; for your light has come! And the glory of the Lord is risen upon you. For behold, the darkness shall cover the earth, and deep darkness the people; but the Lord will arise over you, and His glory will be seen upon you" (Isa. 60:1–2, NKJV).

7. I believe that we are headed into the final great harvest, but that we are not yet crossing over into it.

8. "Among the prophets and teachers of the church at Antioch were Barnabas and Symeon (also called 'The Black Man'), Lucius (from Cyrene), Manaen (the foster-brother of King Herod), and Paul. One day as these men were worshiping and fasting the Holy Spirit said, 'Dedicate Barnabas and Paul for a special job I have for them.' So after more fasting and prayer, the men laid their hands on them—and sent them on their way" (Acts 13:1–3, TLB).

OTHER BOOKS
BY JAMES W. GOLL

(Many titles feature a matching study guide
as well as audio and video presentations.)

Adventures in the Prophetic (coauthors, Michal Ann Goll, Mickey
Robinson, Patricia King, Jeff Jansen, and Ryan Wyatt)

Angelic Encounters (coauthor, Michal Ann Goll)

The Call of the Elijah Revolution (coauthor, Lou Engle)

The Coming Israel Awakening

Deliverance from Darkness

The Discerner

Discovering the Seer in You

Dream Language (coauthor, Michal Ann Goll)

Empowered Prayer

Exploring the Nature and Gift of Dreams

Fearless and Free (coauthor, Michal Ann Goll)

Exploring Your Dreams and Visions

Finding Hope

God Encounters (coauthor, Michal Ann Goll)

God Encounters Today (coauthor, Michal Ann Goll)

Hearing God's Voice Today

Intercession: The Power and Passion to Shape History

James W. Goll 365-Day Personal Prayer Guide

Kneeling on the Promises

The Lifestyle of a Prophet

The Lifestyle of a Watchman

The Lost Art of Intercession

The Lost Art of Practicing His Presence

The Lost Art of Pure Worship (coauthor and contributors, Chris Dupré, Jeff Deyo, Sean Feucht, Julie Meyer)

Living a Supernatural Life

Passionate Pursuit

Prayer Storm

Praying for Israel's Destiny

Praying With God's Heart

The Prophetic Intercessor

A Radical Faith

Releasing Spiritual Gifts Today

The Seer (and *The Seer Expanded*)

The Seer Devotional Journal

Shifting Shadows of Supernatural Experiences (coauthor, Julia Loren)

Strike the Mark

Women on the Frontlines series: A Call to Compassion, A Call to Courage, A Call to the Secret Place (Michal Ann Goll, with James W. Goll)

ABOUT THE AUTHOR

James W. Goll is the founder of God Encounters Ministries. He is also the founder of Prayer Storm and the Worship City Alliance, as well as co-founder of Women on the Frontlines and Compassion Acts. James is a member of the Harvest International Ministries Apostolic Team, the Apostolic Council of Prophetic Elders, and the Bethel Leaders Network. He serves as a core instructor at Wagner University and Christian Leadership University.

After pastoring in the Midwest United States, James was thrust into the role of an international equipper and trainer. He has traveled to over fifty nations, carrying a passion for Jesus wherever he goes. His desire is to see the Body of Christ become the house of prayer for all nations and be empowered by the Holy Spirit to spread the Good News of Jesus to every country and to all peoples.

James teaches online classes and hosts a number of webinars each year. He produces the God Encounters Today podcast with the Charisma Podcast Network, along with a corresponding weekly blog post. Through God Encounters Ministries, he also releases E-Blasts each month, with audio and video messages as well.

James and Michal Ann Goll were married for thirty-two years before her graduation to Heaven in the fall of 2008. James has four married adult children and a growing number of grandchildren. He continues to make his home in Franklin, Tennessee.

FOR MORE INFORMATION

JAMES W. GOLL

God Encounters Ministries
P.O. Box 1653
Franklin, TN 37065
Phone: 1–877–200–1604

Websites:

www.godencounters.com • www.jamesgoll.com

Emails:

info@godencounters.com • invitejames@godencounters.com

Social Media:

Follow James on

Facebook, Instagram, Twitter, XP Media, GEM Media,

Kingdom Flame, YouTube, Vimeo, Charisma Blog, and iTunes

For More Information

James W. Goll

God Encounters Ministries
P.O. Box 1653
Franklin, TN 37065
Phone: 1–877–200–1604

Websites:

www.godencounters.com • www.jamesgoll.com

Emails:

info@godencounters.com • invitejames@godencounters.com

Social Media:

Follow James on

Facebook, Instagram, Twitter, XP Media, GEM Media,

Kingdom Flame, YouTube, Vimeo, Charisma Blog, and iTunes

Experience a personal revival!

Spirit-empowered content from today's top Christian authors delivered directly to your inbox.

Join today!
lovetoreadclub.com

Inspiring Articles
Powerful Video Teaching
Resources for Revival

Get all of this and so much more, e-mailed to you twice weekly!

LOVE TO READ CLUB
by **D DESTINY IMAGE**